TAILS FROM THE BARK SIDE

Brian Kilcommons and
Sarah Wilson

D0039768

WARNER BOOKS

A Time Warner Company

WARNER BOOKS EDITION

Copyright © 1997 by Brian Kilcommons and Sarah Wilson
All rights reserved.

Warner Books, Inc., 1271 Avenue of the Americas, New York, NY 10020

Vist our Web site at www.twbookmark.com.

For information on Time Warner Trade Publishing's online publishing program, vist www.ipublish.com.

 A Time Warner Company

Printed in the United States of America

Originally published in hardcover by Warner Books, Inc.

First Trade Printing: July 2001

10 9 8 7 6 5 4 3 2 1

The Library of Congress has cataloged the hardcover edition as follows:

Kilcommons, Brian.
Tails from the bark side / Brian Kilcommons and Sarah Wilson.
    p.   cm.
ISBN 0-446-52150-7
  1. Dogs—United States—Anecdotes. 2. Dogs—Behavior—United States—Anecdotes. 3. Kilcommons, Brian. 4. Animal trainers—United States—Biography. I. Wilson, Sarah, 1960- . II. Title.
SF426.2.K54   1997
636.7'0887—dc21   97-13196
                                                     CIP

ISBN 0-446-67614-4 (pbk.)

Cover design by Claire Brown
Cover photograph by Nawrocki Stock Photo, Inc.

 **To our friends and families**

Your support, humor, insight, and love
continue to make these books possible.

Acknowledgments

We would like to thank all our clients, both four-footed and two-footed, for making this book possible. All the events in this book are 100 percent true. Names have been changed and details tweaked for privacy reasons. This being the case, please observe the following: If a story is flattering and sounds the tiniest bit like you, we promise it's you! If the story is not flattering and sounds a ton like you, we promise it's someone else.

Introduction

We cannot imagine a day without the muzzle of a cherished canine resting on a knee, the thump of a happy tail when we first open our eyes in the morning, or the sigh of a blissful dog curling up next to us on the couch. (Yes, our dogs are invited up on the furniture more than you might think.)

Dogs are and have always been our playmates, friends, teachers, guardians, and comforters. They are our windows into ourselves, the world around us, and even, for passing glimpses, the unique world they inhabit.

We hope the stories we tell here give you a window into our world. Our lives have been full and, at times, complicated. To make the narrative (and cast of characters, both human and canine) easier to follow, we offer a brief outline of our individual histories.

Brian

Brian grew up on Long Island, New York. He had Irish, a terrier mix, then T., a Vizsla. In his high school years, he worked with dog-show handlers and for a veterinarian. Prevet was next at Iowa State (with T.). Brian worked construction on the side to earn money, then contracted mononucleosis and ran out of cash. He came home and tied steel on the Shoreham Nuclear Plant on Long Island. T. died of cancer. Brian decided that he did not want to spend his life tying steel. After apprenticing with several trainers, he started his own training business, Kilcommons Professional Dog Training, Ltd. Next came Beau, Brian's Rottweiler. Brian met Barbara Woodhouse and became a much better trainer. He met his first wife while training her dog. They got married. Brian became a reporter on animal issues for WABC, then for the CBS morning news. His marriage split up. Next came the ASPCA, where he was the director of training and behavior. Beau also died of cancer.

Sarah

Sarah grew up around Boston, Massachusetts. Her parade of childhood pets included gerbils, hamsters, guinea pigs, rabbits, frogs, toads, snakes, cats, and finches. She rode horses, then helped train them. She became smitten with Firefly, a lively Morgan/Arabian cross. After her folks divorced, Sarah and her mother moved to St. Louis. (Firefly had to be sold prior to the move.) After many years of begging, her mother finally said yes to a dog, so a little mixed breed named Butterfly joined the ranks. Itching to work with more animals, Sarah started training a few dogs of friends and neighbors, which was interrupted by her attending Amherst College. After graduation, Sarah sold shoes, then worked with troubled teens. She met her first husband, Peter. While living with Peter, she acquired Sasha, a field-bred English Springer Spaniel. Sarah and Peter married, then moved to Manhattan. Kesl, a Bouvier des Flandres, came into her life at that point. Sarah worked at an art gallery full-time while she developed her training business at nights and on the weekends. They moved to Brooklyn, New York. During this time, Sarah started Paws to Consider Dog Training. After almost dying from a ruptured appendix, she evaluated her life, quit her secure job, divorced her husband, and started training full-time.

Brian and Sarah Together

Sarah and Brian met and became fast friends. After meeting Brian, Sarah became a much better trainer. They lived together in Brooklyn, then Long Island, New York. Combining their two separate businesses, they formed The Family Dog, Inc. Piper, a Scottish Deerhound, joined the family. They moved to Manhattan to open The Family Dog Training Center. Caras, an Australian Shepherd, was the next addition. Brian and Sarah left the city, moving to Middletown, New York. They got Julia, a German Shepherd; Cedie, another Aussie; Emily, a sweet, abandoned female cat; and Ben, a burly, abused kitten. Brian and Sarah collaborated on *Good Owners, Great Dogs; Childproofing Your Dog;* and *Good Owners, Great Cats.* Brian started teaching electives on training and behavior at Tufts University School of Veterinary Medicine. They moved to Canterbury Farm, where they both hope to stay for many years. Their next project was *Mutts: America's Dogs,* written with Mike Capuzzo. Brian and Sarah watch over two horses, a flock of chickens, and a growing number of sheep. Urs, another German Shepherd, and Lucy, a wild orange kitten, recently joined the menagerie. After nearly a decade together, Brian and Sarah married. They are now in the process of living happily ever after.

In some ways, having a canine companion is the simplest thing in the world. All they need is love, exercise, training, care, and shelter. In other ways, it requires a leap of faith by both parties to make it work. Dogs must believe that we can make some sense of a confusing world; that we have the answers to their questions, if they listen.

For our part, we must build the bridge between the dog and ourselves—using trust, kindness, consistency, and patience to do so. We are their guides, a job that requires careful attention to our own urges to control, give up, wield power, or be passive.

Working with animals bares our own monsters. The dogs see them all. If we are afraid to be leaders, the dogs will not believe in us. If we are intoxicated by control, our dogs will not trust. If we do not take the job of teaching seriously, our dogs will not follow. If we think them stupid, they will behave stupidly. If we mistake anger for teaching, they will teach us the price exacted on their soul and ours.

Our canine companions elicit almost every emotion life has to offer—tenderness as we look down at our sleeping puppy's face, frustration when a dog is a dog despite our efforts to stop them, joy when they greet us at the door, grief when they leave us all too soon, rage when we think they have defied us, glee when we romp together with total abandon. And everything we offer them, they accept—good, bad, or indifferent. Rarely can we claim to do the same. No matter how much we project our beliefs about what a dog is onto their furry bodies, they are, in the end, themselves—perfect and perfectly charming, outside our understanding perhaps, but deeply within our hearts.

TAILS FROM THE BARK SIDE

CANINE COMEDIANS

Dropping the Ball (SARAH)

Jack Russell Terriers are characters—it doesn't matter whether they are male or female, young or old—they all have strong opinions about life and their place in it. Fourteen-pound Tank was no exception. He loved a lot of things in life—"his" children, rawhides, chasing squirrels, anything that flew, a good long walk in the morning. But his obsession, his great and terrible love, was an old, ratty, orange tennis ball.

Mary and Richard had always thought this tennis ball mania endearing, until they started to renovate their home. As part of that remodeling, they added a forced-air heating system.

One day, upon returning from yet another trip to the hardware store, they heard Tank barking frantically upstairs. Something was wrong! Alarmed, they raced up to help him. There he stood, barking nonstop down a brand-new, as-yet-uncovered heating duct. Was he frightened of it? Was he imagining some terrier nightmare about large animals down dark holes? Picking him up, Richard soothed him. "There, there Tank. Calm down. That's just a heat duct, nothing to be scared of." Richard carried him downstairs, but Tank had other plans. He struggled free, then raced back to the duct and took up where he had left off.

Under normal circumstances, Jack Russell barking is no easy thing to listen to—it is loud, can be high-pitched, and is usually rapid fire. Now, imagine it echoing down long metal ductwork and you can see the problem. Tank sounded like a canine machine gun that never needed reloading. He kept at it—ten minutes stretched to twenty. He showed no sign of letting up. A focused terrier is an astonishing thing.

Desperate, Mary and Richard decided to distract him with his favorite toy. But where was it? Where was his beloved tennis ball? Slowly, it dawned on them. The ball must have rolled down the open duct.

The only solution was to call in the heating professional. Yes, he would be glad to come out. It would be an emergency call, of course. Tank barked until the heating expert arrived. He barked while the man scrambled into the crawl space under their home, made his way to the lowest part of the ductwork, then cut it. Out rolled the grimy ball. The repairman closed up the opening before crawling back out to hand the offending ball and the hefty bill to Richard. But Richard didn't mind. The ball was back. All was well with his world.

"Poor Tanky," Richard commiserated, "you lost your favorite toy. But we rescued it. Here you go!" and he tossed the ball into the air. Richard smiled as Tank caught it on the first bounce. Turning to Mary, Richard said with a grin, "He's happy now!" Tank bolted from the room. They heard canine toenails scrambling up wooden stairs. "Oh no." Richard groaned. "He wouldn't . . ." Then the house reverberated with the sound of a soft orb bouncing down a long metal tract—*whomp, whomp, whomp, whomp*. A sound that was instantly obscured by Tank's gleeful barking.

Wanted: Gardeners (BRIAN)

The estate Murphy reigned over was built by Thomas Jefferson, who I am sure would have been impressed by the dog if he had met him. Encompassing over one hundred acres of the greenest Virginia countryside, the century-old plantings needed constant attention to stay at their most beautiful. The skills of many gardeners were required. A problem arose when Mrs. Roswell, the owner, could no longer find people willing to take on the work. Murphy was making hiring impossible.

Murphy, an unneutered male Rottweiler, was never what you would call a nice dog. Loyal to the bone to the few people he loved, he considered all other humans lesser forms of life. Being highly intelligent, he made up a game that quickly became his favorite. Here are the rules: Wait out of sight until gardener bends over, absorbed in his or her work. Proceeding slowly, with stealth, sneak up behind aforementioned human. Do not pant or make noise of any kind. Come close to gardener's rear end, inches if possible, ideally right where the legs meet the body. Inhale deeply. Bark as loudly as possible.

If all goes well, human will shoot forward into bush or leap upward in a most satisfying way. If he or she has a good sense of humor about it all, strut away, mouth open, tongue lolling, with an ear-to-ear Rottweiler grin. If human attempts to reprimand you, swell up to one and a half times your normal size, make direct eye contact, and growl so deeply that he or she feels it through their feet.

If intimidation is successful, human will freeze, blanch, and gasp in the most wonderful way. Maintain position for a minute or more, then slowly turn and stalk off. Hike leg on nearest vertical object. Scrape hind paws repeatedly after urination, ideally tossing bits of leaves and grass at the motionless human. If done properly, human will quit job.

As his owner worshiped the ground he walked on but had neither the temperament nor the interest to firmly manage his dog, Murphy pretty much did what he wanted. I did work with the head gardener, which gave him some influence over the dog, but I would never have called it control.

But things came to a head when the estate's small barn needed reshingling and two workmen, Tom and Jeremy, came to do the job. The barn stood, quaint and picturesque, off in a back glen. As the sun lifted slowly into the clear Virginia sky, Murphy discovered the interlopers up on *his* roof.

The young men had just hauled two bundles of shingles up to the roof, and Jeremy was starting down the ladder for a third bundle, when he noticed the black hulk asleep at the foot of the ladder. "Big dog," he muttered to himself. Murphy simply raised his basketball-like head and watched.

When Jeremy got within a few feet of the ground, Murphy's eyes narrowed. A deep rumbling could be heard. At first, the roofer thought that a distant train was making its way to some unknown destination. Then he realized from whence it actually came. Jeremy froze, foot extended toward earth. Murphy rose slowly, eyes locked on the intruder. As the workman cautiously started his ascent to safety, Murphy launched, lips pulled back, primitive noises erupting from his gut. Spurred by fear and adrenaline, Jeremy climbed to the roof nimbly as a schoolboy. There the two men stood, shaking, looking for escape. There was none. The black asphalt-shingled roof was their lifeboat and below Murphy circled the barn like a great white shark.

Out of everyone's earshot, the workmen's yells for help went unheard. Resigned, they sat down to develop a plan. Their first thought was to distract the dog. Tom went to the far side of the building and made noise by banging his hammer against the roof. Instantly, Murphy galloped over to check out the commotion. With the dog distracted, the faster of the two men, Jeremy, started down the ladder. In his haste, the metal ladder banged against the barn. Tom just had time to yell, "He's coming!" before Murphy arrived, barking like Cerberus guarding the gates of hell and leaping up against the ladder. Jeremy sprinted to safety.

Both men peered over the side at the massive creature. "Jesus," Tom said. "That was a little too close."

"No kidding," Jeremy replied. "Got any other bright ideas? Preferably something that wouldn't involve me being eaten?"

"Think we can scare him off? Maybe throw something at him?" his friend offered.

"Like what? You got an H-bomb in your pocket?" Jeremy shook his head. "We'll just have to wait him out." And with that he lay back on the roof, pulled his jacket over his face for some shade, and pretended to sleep.

The sun heated the dark roof quickly. The men's T-shirts, saturated with sweat, stuck to their skin. Murphy, cool in the shade of the barn, planted himself at the bottom of the ladder and napped. He knew that the men would have to go past him to leave. They knew it, too.

All day they waited, stranded on that roof. Periodically they called out for help, but nobody heard them. Sometimes they talked, mostly about the six-pack of beer that sat heating up in their truck and the pack of cigarettes in the glove compartment. They both agreed, eventually, the dog would forget about them and leave. Neither had ever met Murphy.

As the sun slowly slipped across the horizon, the roofers renewed their bellowing. The farm manager, Ed, was leaving the horse barn when he heard a distant sound. He couldn't quite make it out. He hopped in his truck and rolled down his window so he could follow the noise. Down the hill, through the small grove, it seemed to be coming from the small barn.

Pulling in the drive, he immediately understood the situation. He opened the door of his Chevy and called the dog to him. Murphy hopped in, rubbing his massive head against his friend, inadvertently shoving him against the inside of the car door in his enthusiasm. Kept 'em for you, boss! he seemed to say.

With Murphy safely locked in the truck, Tom and Jeremy climbed down, collected their things, got a day's wages each, and left. The farm could keep the new shingles on the roof; neither man cared to go up and retrieve them.

Pick on Someone Your Own Size (BRIAN)

Being small is much more a problem of external perception than of internal reality, or so Bon Bon would tell you if he could. At 5 pounds, 0 ounces this Maltese Poodle mix has a soul that is a combination of kamikaze fighter, trapeze artist, and political dictator.

Boarded with a friend, Lara, who keeps a few client dogs in her home on occasion, Bon Bon takes all comers. As Lara told Bon Bon's owners, "If this dog was 65 pounds, you wouldn't be able to keep him."

But he isn't, so his owners think his antics are charming, rather than dangerous. Because of his size and potential vulnerability to unintended injury, Lara placed Bon Bon in the kitchen behind a wrought-iron gate. There he could safely watch everything going on.

Enter Flint, a large Shepherd-Collie cross. Bon Bon immediately barked his challenge. Flint, a true saint among dogs, ignored this onslaught.

Bon Bon took only a second to slip between the bars of the gate, which had held all manner of tiny dogs before him.

A fluffy coat can make even small dogs appear larger than they are.

Bon Bon launched himself at Flint's face, spitting canine cuss words at the top of his voice. Flint simply raised his head and regarded Bon Bon with a bemused expression that seemed to say, "Kid, you've got chutzpah . . . no brains but a lot of chutzpah."

Such benevolence further infuriated the tiny warrior. Determined to get the desired results, Bon Bon raced behind Flint. Leaping into the air, he caught Flint's tail and hung on. Once his four feet touched the ground, he threw everything he had into reverse. Tugging, growling fiercely, shaking his head back and forth, he defied Flint to ignore him. Eyes widened briefly in surprise, Flint strolled off, pulling Bon Bon behind like a miniature water-skier.

Bon Bon met his match one day in a Welsh Corgi named Watson. Having done his best to impress Watson and receiving the usual unsatisfactory response, Bon Bon lit out for his usual target. Reaching his goal, he scrambled to a stop. No tail. Cocking his head for a second, Bon Bon improvised and grabbed Watson's fluffy britches.

Watson spun around and with his right front paw gently pressed Bon Bon to the ground. Bon Bon struggled for a few seconds until Watson leaned in and growled softly. The effect was immediate. Bon Bon could not have been more still if he had died of surprise.

Satisfied, Watson slowly removed his paw, gazed upon the motionless Bon Bon for another second, then went off about his business. Bon Bon lay still. He rolled his eyes left, then right, scanning for the larger dog. Cautiously he raised his head. When he saw the coast was clear, he got up, shook himself off, and retreated to the kitchen.

Watson did his job well. To this day, if he even looks sideways at the little dog, Bon Bon falls over and plays dead until his lord and master moves away.

Not My Type (SARAH)

In the last shot of the day, a canine masseuse was to be filmed working her magic on Caras as he lay, stretched out, half-asleep, on a red velvet couch. Great idea for a TV show about indulging one's canine companion in Manhattan.

Caras's job did not appear difficult—relax, close eyes, enjoy the moment. I set him up on the couch, a place he was more than happy to be. He plunked down, mouth open, eyes bright. What's next? he seemed to be saying. He was ready.

Enter Margot, a slender, longhaired woman in a long, floral-print cotton dress. She was the costar of the segment, a canine massage professional. Nervous, talking with the director about the scene, she ignored my suggestions about how to get acquainted with my dog. Plopping herself down on the couch next to Caras with no introduction, she put her hands on him immediately.

Caras's reaction to this was not much different from what yours might be if a stranger sat down in your space and placed his hands on you without introduction. Caras hopped right off, with a glance over his shoulder that roughly translated, Who the heck is that?

Now there is something you should know about Australian Shepherds. Once they form an opinion about someone, it is hard to change their minds. Impossible to change would be a more honest statement. My stomach tightened: I knew all the ramifications of what had just happened.

I asked Margot to get up for a minute to greet Caras formally. He stood politely as she offered a hand for him, but he would not sniff it. He would not look at her. Hopping back up on the couch at my command, he lay back down. I told him to stay. She sat back down. He rolled so his back faced her, burying his head into the corner of the cushions. I sighed. Just as I thought.

The director looked at me questioningly. Caras had been nothing but easy and reliable during the other shots the show required. I shrugged. "Why don't you do a little of your massage on him to relax him?" I suggested, in hopes that her skills might influence his opinion.

She placed her delicate hands on his shoulders and started to knead him as if he were a mass of very stiff dough. He squirmed. "He's sensitive," I said, though I wanted to say, You idiot! This is a dog, not a loaf of bread in the making. Gentle! Can't you see he doesn't like what you're doing?

"Okay," said the director. "Sarah, get Caras turned around.

Margot, get ready." Once her hands were off his back, I used treats and sweet talk to get him in the right position. After a few moments of stroking, to relax him, I gave him a no-nonsense "Stay," backing away just out of camera range.

Margot placed her hands on him again. As she spoke her lines, her nervousness came through her hands. She massaged faster, harder. Caras looked at me. I put my hand up, signaling him firmly to stay. He sighed, then rolled on his side, wrapped his hind legs behind her, and pushed with all his might. If I have to stay, he clearly was thinking, you have to go!

Raking his hind feet across the small of her flimsy cotton-covered back, he pushed her again and again. Arching her back in an attempt to avoid this onslaught, she continued with her lines as best she could. Finally, as her squirming and his kicking reached a fevered pitch, the director yelled, "Cut!" Caras shot off the couch, diving under a small coffee table. Facing the wall, he stuck his furry butt out for all to see. His feelings about this whole process were clear.

Margot glared at me. "Make him stop!" she demanded. A slow smile spread across my face. "He'll stop when he's relaxed. Isn't getting a dog to relax kind of your department?" Turning to the director, I apologized. "There seems to be a . . . problem." He nodded at this statement of the obvious.

"Suggestions?" he asked.

"Well, since Caras clearly isn't wild about this scene, why don't we do this—I'll sit in for Margot. Get the close-ups of the body work being done, using my hands. If I push my sleeves up, I'll have bare arms like hers. Then we'll do the interview with Margot sitting next to Caras but not working on him." This seemed worth trying.

With Margot out of sight in another room, Caras happily hopped back up on the couch. I worked on him gently. His eyes closing, his body relaxed in contentment. Once he was near sleep, Margot quietly took up her spot next to him. With her hands resting gently on his shoulders, the scene was shot.

When it was over, Margot left thinking I didn't know much about controlling my dog and I left thinking she didn't know much about doggy massage. Caras was clearly the winner here. He got exactly what he wanted.

His Smile Almost Killed Him (BRIAN)

One afternoon, we got a call from Barbara, one of our favorite breeders. Her Standard Poodles have some of the most predictably rock-solid temperaments we've ever had the pleasure of working with, largely because she herself is terrified of aggression. In fact, she is nervous around many dogs. Anything with the slightest hint of nastiness is eliminated from her breeding program immediately. This zero-tolerance rule means that her dogs, like no one's I've ever seen, are a happy, low-key bunch who don't even have a place in their head for words like *aggression, unstable, mean, unreliable, possessive.*

When she called, Barbara was distraught. A family who had one of her dogs reported to her from the Southwest that their poodle, Sport, was *aggressive*!

This nice family had done all the right things. They had hired two different trainers, both of whom confirmed the fact that this dog was unmanageable: snarling at the door, leaping and snarling at strangers, a whirling dervish around other dogs.

In disbelief, hoping this wasn't true, I called the owners myself to get the story firsthand. Yes, it was all true, and it got worse. Not only was he proclaimed dangerous but the trainers had been unable to stop his aggressive displays. When they corrected him, he continued to snarl at them. Unbelievable! Horrifying! How was this possible?

Over the years, Sarah and I have become increasingly convinced that temperament is genetically based. If an individual from a family of dogs rigorously selected for non-aggression could develop such aberrant behavior, then we would have to rethink our conclusions. We considered every option. Perhaps an illness could be causing this behavior. Maybe a brain tumor?

The family loved the dog but did not feel they could keep him. The trainers were recommending euthanasia. Barbara was beside herself. Could we please, please take a look at this dog? She had to know, not just for his sake but for the sake of her whole breeding program. Of course we would look at him. And in he flew from New Mexico to our little kennel in upstate New York

It was with extreme caution that I looked inside that

crate for the first time. Speaking softly, I bent over and introduced myself. The plastic crate reverberated with the thumps of Sport's happy tail. Ah, this was like Barbara's dogs! A glimmer of hope was kindled. Maybe . . .

Opening the crate a bit, I slipped on a lead and out stepped a stunning black dog typical of Barbara's breeding—happy, personable, elegant—and then it happened. He showed every tooth in his head.

Gasping with surprise, I hesitated, and then I burst out laughing. This wasn't aggression. Sport was smiling. Called in the training world a submissive grin, in human terms it meant, Hey, how're you doing? I'm a really nice guy. He had the biggest grin we'd ever seen, a virtual canine Howdy Doody. His set of pearly whites against his pitch-black face was striking.

He did leap, barking and grinning at other dogs, but he just wanted to meet them. He did leap, snorting and grinning when people entered the house, but all in the best of fun. Of course, the more the trainers had corrected him for this "aggression," the more submissive he had become. Figuring they were missing the point of his display—and he was right about that—he grinned more. The more he grinned, the more he got corrected. He had come within a hair's breadth of smiling himself to death.

We kept him for a few weeks just to make sure nothing evil lurked in the recesses of Sport's mind. This dog would not have understood evil if you had tried to explain it to him. Then the poodle-rescue network placed him in a wonderful home, where he now lives, much adored, tail wagging and teeth flashing.

Are You Done Yet? (SARAH)

Some clients in this business make you feel wonderful. Sherry and Rick, a couple from Long Island, were such clients. They researched the breed they wanted, interviewed breeders, got the puppy, called me, practiced the training, followed the advice, and came out of it all with a wonderful German Shepherd female, Heidi. When I think of great Shepherds I have known, she always springs to mind.

Early on, I saw signs of how special she was. During puppy training, which is basically structured fun and games, we were working on establishing a joyful recall, which means the dog comes when called. If you teach a dog early to enjoy coming to you, to feel as though he is being allowed to come, not just that he has to come, you are halfway to an instant, joyful recall for the rest of his life. One of the games I had Sherry and Rick play was to wait till Heidi was out of sight, then call her to them with much clapping and praise. When she arrived and sat, she would get a treat and be fussed over. Heidi loved this game!

As the days progressed, Sherry noticed that Heidi was coming faster and faster. Not only that; the pup was scooting out of the room more and more. Her speed of response was miraculous—suspiciously miraculous. Sherry set her up. When Heidi trotted out of the room on her stubby little puppy legs, Sherry sneaked after her. Peeking around the corner, what did she find? Heidi, sitting pressed into the hall corner by the door, obediently waiting just out of sight to be called.

This may seem like a simple thing, but it is a level of problem solving seldom seen in dogs. She had to realize what was going to happen, then arrange it so she could make it happen over and over again. Such canine intellect arises from a combination of good genetics, careful rearing by a conscientious breeder, and early teaching by committed owners.

As Heidi grew, so did her comprehension. When last I spoke to Sherry and Rick, Heidi had tricked them again.

They were in the habit of giving Heidi all the crusts of pizzas they ate. Heidi liked this routine a great deal, sitting quietly by the table waiting for them to finish.

One night, after sharing a pepperoni and mushroom pizza in the living room, Sherry and Rick got into a heated discussion about politics. As the minutes wore on, they completely forgot to toss Heidi her patiently awaited share. Sudden barking interrupted their bickering. Heidi was hysterical by the front door, lunging at the glass, leaving trails of saliva across the panes. They rushed to turn on the light and see what was causing this intense response. They peered into the dark: nothing. Rick stepped outside for a better look: nothing. Then they noticed that their gallant watchdog was not with them. Going back to the living room, they found her curled up on her bed, asleep. Not a pizza crust was left in the box.

Mission accomplished.

Chemical Warfare (BRIAN)

A national TV show invited me to discuss photographing one's dog. I brought Beau, my Rottweiler, along as my demo dog.

It amazes me what we all tolerate from our dogs. What we would throw a spouse out of the room for immediately, and with much verbal haranguing, we smile and take as a matter of course with our pets. I am no exception. Beau's intestinal gas could wake you out of a sound sleep and make you wish you were dead. Everything about this 130-pound animal was formidable, and his emissions were no exception. Usually, this problem occurred only in the evening, but not always.

At any TV studio, the greenroom is the place where guests wait before they go on the air. Usually, it isn't actually green. I don't know where the name originated. It's just a room with a couch, a couple of chairs, a coffeepot, a plateful of delicious treats, and a bunch of nervous people about to sit in front of a camera.

Given what talkative people television personalities are, most greenrooms are surprisingly quiet. Whether it's nerves or what, I cannot tell you. But this day was no different. I parked Beau out of the way, behind a chair, then settled in to wait for my turn on-set.

While thumbing through an outdated copy of *Time* magazine, I heard a telltale sound, a quiet *psst*, like some tiny librarian hushing me. Before I could turn to look at Beau, I got olfactory confirmation of what had just happened. It was a sound I would hear several more times in the next ten minutes.

When I peered around the chair at my big lug, he lifted his huge head, put his ears back, and wagged his stump. Hi. Something you want from me? he seemed to say. I sighed, leaning back in my chair, my eyes watering from the stench. I considered giving him a quick walk, but the street was an elevator ride away; I might not make it back in time for my segment. This was a live show; missing a segment was not an option.

In hindsight, I guess I could have taken him into the hall, but such an obvious action didn't occur to me. It was just one of those moments when mortification slows down the thought process. My mind was pretty much filled with the thought, This cannot be happening.

By this time, the fog of stink had made its way across the room. Several people who had entered after me—a well-known soap-opera star, a chef, and a country singer—could not see Beau behind my chair. What they did know was someone in the room had a very serious problem. No one was talking; no one was making eye contact. It's one of those awkward social moments. You know you didn't do it. You hope other people don't think you did it, but asking around about who cut this amazing stink is hardly conversationally correct. People lit cigarettes; one woman bravely reapplied her perfume. I looked around for a window to crack. There was none. Not that any of this made a tremendous difference. It was like throwing a thimbleful of water at an inferno.

Employees from all over the building always raid the greenroom's plate of goodies. Several of these unfortunates entered the room with the speed and confidence of habit, only to stop dead several strides away from their goal. Emotions flitted across their features—surprise, disgust—then, glancing at the guests, they muttered to themselves—"Oh, I forgot, I have to . . ." and fled.

At about that time, the door swung open and a pert, smiling eighteen-year-old aide made way for Mrs. Mario Cuomo to enter the room. We all turned toward the fresh air let in by the open door. The aide flashed a blinding smile, bubbling to the governor's wife, "You'll find what you need in—" As she stepped into the room to hold the door for her guest, she froze. She gasped slightly, her lovely smile turning to a death-mask grimace.

Elegant Mrs. Cuomo, a step or two behind the aide, hit the offensive sensory experience next. Pulling herself upright, eyes narrowing, she scanned the room like an accusing schoolteacher. Her glare landed on the soap star. Horrified, he shook his head in denial, but she had already found him guilty. Pivoting on her heel, she left. The aide gratefully followed. The door closed slowly, allowing one last puff of fresh air into our swamp before it shut.

The soap star turned three shades of red. The country singer, who was sitting next to him, rose, got a cup of coffee, then chose a chair across the room. I heard Beau sigh softly as he shifted slightly behind the chair. Praying that he had released all he had to give this day, I picked up the battered magazine, pretending to read. I would admit to nothing, not if I could help it.

Indefatigable (SARAH)

Cedie, our Australian Shepherd female, is a nutcase, and this is from the woman who loves her best. If she were a child, I might say she has poor impulse control, perhaps even attention deficit disorder.

She reacts to most everything. Every noise, every person, every situation, even every chemical in her environment causes strong responses. She is, by nature, a barker, using her voice as punctuation, exclamation, and general expression. She barks in alarm, in joy, in excitement, in concern. The pitch of that bark falls somewhere between a car alarm and fingernails on a chalkboard. She is the Fran Drescher of the canine world. As annoying as she is, she is also one of the brightest dogs I have ever met, and I've met thousands.

Here are a few typical moments in Cedie's history.

It took Cedie a long time to grasp the concept of *around*, as in to go around something. If she was in the hall when I called her, she came to me in a straight line—over the back of the couch, one bounce off the seat cushions, into the middle of the coffee table (usually scattering magazines), then, in one smooth vault, landing in my lap. Now, what do I say to that? She *did* come and it was immediate, enthusiastic, and happy—can't correct *that*.

She treated our other dogs similarly. If called from a distance, she would jump over, scoot under, or use the backs of our older dogs as a vaulting platform on her way to my side. This is dangerous business. Dogs often regard paws on their back as a challenge. Lucky for Cedie, she moves close to the speed of sound. She was always long gone before her involuntary pommel horse realized what had happened, leaving the surprised victim snapping at air.

Though Cedie annoys me often, she makes me laugh even more. When she was a young pup, maybe nine weeks old, I went to put her in her crate so I could go out and do errands. She was chewing on a bone at the time. When she saw me coming, she looked at me, then the bone, then at me again. When I reached down to scoop her up, she grasped the bone between her front paws. As I carried her to her crate, she carried her bone. I made a detour to show Brian, who was, as he usually is, on the phone. I held her out in front of me, her grasp on the bone firm. His eyebrows lifted slightly. "This is not good news," I commented. He nodded agreement.

Intelligence in dogs is a double-edged blade. Most people

are much better off with a slightly dull but sweet dog. Intelligence is a burden because smart dogs, problem solvers like Cedie, are prone to getting into trouble of all sorts. Cedie has proved that to be true many times over.

Quite soon after the bone-holding incident, I watched her figure out another mystery. She was leaping up at the cat, who was curled up on an afghan (blanket—not dog) on the couch. Cedie was determined to make contact, but her short puppy legs did not allow her to reach the cat. She sat for a moment, staring up at the couch. Then, grasping the edge of the blanket that hung over the couch cushion, she backed up, tugging and yanking until she pulled the blanket and thus the cat to the edge. Once the cat was in sight, she released the blanket and, with a bark, launched herself at her unwilling playmate.

Cedie specializes in doing the unexpected. When asked to get into the car as an older pup, she leapt from a standstill onto the roof, where she waggled with enthusiasm. Once when a good friend of the family, and one of Cedie's major fans, stopped by for a visit, Cedie raced up to her car, barking nonstop. Seeing who it was, she broke into intense whining and leapt through the half-open window on the driver's side, muddy paws and all, to say hello. Another friend, who was paddling around her pond on an inflatable raft at the time, made the mistake of saying Cedie's name. Cedie instantly launched herself in a stunning arc and landed with her full weight on one side of my friend's flotation device. The raft, never meant to handle these circumstances, tilted wildly under Cedie's weight. She raced around barking while my friend yelled and I laughed.

If Cedie could say one thing in her life, I am quite sure it would be, Gravity is a bummer. She lives to be airborne. It took me one session to teach her to leap onto my back to vault into the air to catch a Frisbee. I have yet to learn to throw it properly, but she has really gotten the knack for vaulting. Here, her incredible speed and fearlessness are assets. I even had to teach her to loop behind me before heading out for a catch, because she was consistently getting out before the Frisbee was anywhere in sight.

She is high-energy, high-maintenance, and always in high spirits. We can direct her, instruct her, train her, and love her, but none of that changes who she is; it just makes her a more controllable version of her indefatigable self.

Catch Me If You Can (BRIAN)

Most terriers have a well-developed sense of humor, frequently at the owner's expense. Gimlet, the Cairn Terrier, was twelve pounds of wirehaired, brindle-colored imp who cohabited (does one ever really "own" a terrier?) with a high-powered CEO of a Fortune 500 company and his equally high-powered wife.

"I'm going to kill Gimlet!" the frustrated, breathless voice shot over the phone.

"Ah, Bob?" I inquired. "What seems to be the problem?"

"If I can catch her, she's dead." I knew he was kidding, but only just. "I have a meeting—*had* a meeting—over an hour ago, but I can't get Gimlet in her crate."

"Can't?" I countered.

"Can't. She won't let me catch her—period. I've been crawling around this apartment for an hour." He sounded utterly deflated.

"Crawling?" I grinned. What an image. Here's a man who has complete control in his work life, crawling after a dog. Priceless. One of the great gifts canines give us is that they don't give a whit about money, status, success, or social position. If you handle a nice dog well, she'll obey adoringly. If you don't, it doesn't much matter if you are the queen of England, the dog just won't listen.

"What's Gimlet doing?" I ventured.

"Honestly? Besides staying just beyond my grasp? It's gonna sound crazy, but I'd say laughing. That dog is laughing at me."

"Ah . . ." I said. "She's a true terrier. The just barely out-of-reach game, I'm familiar with it. Very effective game. Is she barking much?"

"Like a maniac—when I get near, when she bolts off, when she is doing laps around the coffee table . . ." His words faded into a chuckle.

"Terriers love a good chase, remember?" I offered, as we'd had this discussion before. "Are you angry?"

"Am I angry!" His voice rose a notch. "Of course I am angry! She's being a complete little—"

"Bob, take a breath. What starts out as a game becomes something else once you lose your cool. She'll get frightened; then there is no hope of her coming to you or allowing herself to be caught." This was a hard lesson for him, one I was sure Gimlet eventually would teach him. "Okay, Bob? Get a piece of cheese. Sound relaxed and unconcerned; show her the treat and then toss it in the crate. In a happy voice, tell her, 'Kennel.'"

"What will that teach her? I want her to go in automatically." He never liked what he saw as bribes.

"Well, Bob, you're not exactly in a teaching position right now, are you? First, let's contain her; then let's set things up so you have control. When you have control, then you can teach her. Till that time, as you have already noticed, she's in charge, and her idea of fun is to run!" I paused for a second, letting that sink in. "You are, by the way, cooperating with her game plan beautifully." A groan came over the line.

"Okay, I'll do it, but I don't think it will work. . . ." He put down the phone. I could hear the refrigerator door open, and he called her halfheartedly. In a second, I heard the crate door close.

"I hate you," he said, returning to the phone.

"I know." I smiled. "Bob, remember: Control first, then train. Never try to train if you don't have control; all you'll teach her to do is to run away and bark."

"Yeah, yeah. I hate you and I'm late. Thanks, Brian."

"My pleasure, Bob." We hung up. I leaned back in my chair, smiling at the image of Bob in his Italian custom-made suit crawling around his apartment for over an hour while he cursed, pleaded, and yelled as his tiny canine dynamo ran loops around him.

It's hard once you get into a force mode to pull out and try a different way, but it's worth it. As another trainer once said, "How long do you dial a wrong number?" Apparently, Bob's willing to dial for over an hour.

Humble Pie (SARAH)

Dogs never let you get too full of yourself. Just when you think you have a few things figured out, they go and invent a new twist that leaves you shaking your head in puzzlement.

When I was just starting out in the business, I was very much an "in" person—*in*secure, *in*experienced, and, as all beginners are, slightly *in*ept. I worried that my dogs would make mistakes, which they did, and that this would reflect on my training ability, which, I'm sure, it did.

When you live in the city, you can't hide anything. If you can't walk the walk, don't talk the talk, because your dogs will be in the parks and on the streets, where everyone can see them.

Kesl, my Bouvier des Flandres, taught me this. During that nervous beginner's time, he began peeing on people. Lovely—just what my ego needed. This disgusting problem never went unnoticed. The wet recipient would leap back, squawking with surprise. A few of the morning-walk crowd might laugh; others glared at me as I looked for a rock to crawl under. Why couldn't Kesl come up with some other, more easily hidden problem, like eating my shoes in the privacy of our own apartment?

We soon became social pariahs. The moment we appeared, certain people would call their dogs and leave the dog play group without comment, though they weren't above exchanging nasty looks with one another.

This problem is usually not any great mystery. The dog is making a dominance statement, one that is hard to ignore. It is also not unheard-of for adolescent male dogs to do this a time or two when they are in the awkward teen months. But Kesl didn't fit into either profile. In fact, he was the politest of dogs, a true gentleman in all ways. This sudden onset of apparent rudeness was positively confusing. It seemed random—he chose both men and women. It happened only in the park, when many dogs were present. He would walk up casually behind his chosen target, then urinate down the back of their calves. By the time they felt the warmth, it was too late. Kesl was already trotting off jauntily, seemingly pleased with himself, leaving me to wipe off legs while apologizing profusely.

I understood enough about dogs at that time to know that a normally well-behaved, neutered male dog does not just begin this uncharacteristic behavior out of the blue. Something had to be motivating him, but what? I paid close attention to whom he picked.

His actions remained a mystery, until one day it all came together. I was standing around, chatting with the other dog owners in Prospect Park, Brooklyn. Early-morning runs are a major social event for both the dogs and the people. Few groups are as accepting, friendly, and happy as a bunch of people talking about their canine companions. Suddenly, a skirmish broke out. Bill's feisty little Fox Terrier was picking on a young, overly friendly Lab puppy. Within moments, Kesl lined up to soak Bill's leg.

I caught him by the collar, explaining in a clear, firm, unmistakable manner that this was not to happen ever again. He was not to think it. He was not to do it. After I released him, he hung around me for a few minutes, then headed off to explore. I smiled to myself.

I'll never know exactly what Kesl's logic was, but I suspect it went along these lines: Bill's dog is aggressive. I'd rather not fight with Bill's dog, so I claim Bill for my own. In Kesl's world, where humans were always number one, this settled the matter without violence. His choices weren't random at all. He simply marked any owner of a dog who behaved aggressively in the group. I had to give him credit: This was a mighty eloquent liquid statement.

That was the end of Kesl's people-peeing problems. Now that I had cracked the code of his intentions, I could anticipate his actions, then head him off at the pass. If a fight broke out, if I saw him look around the crowd, I'd butt in, saying, "Kess, don't you dare" in a deep, serious tone. He'd drop his head slightly, then trot off, another perfectly good plan foiled, as far as he was concerned.

Coming From Behind (BRIAN)

Most dogs will do anything to get attention. In a busy household, what's critical is to make every effort to avoid rewarding the most obnoxious behavior the dog has to offer. In the world of dog training, if the squeaky wheel gets the grease, it will squeak more. But avoiding doing just that is sometimes easier said than done.

One of my favorite examples of this was Duncan, a wiry thirty-pound Whippet/Lab cross who had way too much time on his hands and not nearly enough exercise. He was the worst thing a young, smart, athletic dog can be—bored.

He lived with four children ranging from ages ten to sixteen, and two parents. The game he made up was rear attack. His thrill in life was sneaking up behind someone and nipping them on the butt. This got him an instantaneous response 100 percent of the time: squealing, then inevitable pursuit, which, to Duncan, was the best part. There isn't a person alive who's going to catch a tight-skinned, well-muscled Whippet cross who does not want to be caught. From Duncan's perspective, people were finally paying attention to him; he got in a good run, albeit indoors— what could be so bad about that? Sure, they were enraged, but that was only a problem if they caught him. Duncan's intelligent answer to that one downside of this entertaining game was simply to avoid getting caught.

As Duncan perfected this pastime, he took to waiting at the bottom of the stairs in ambush. When some poor soul would head for the second floor, he would streak up, nip, and be gone from sight within seconds. This took his game to a dangerous new level, especially if anyone happened to be carrying an armload of stuff.

I got called in. After some basic control was taught to both the humans and the canine, along with serious discussions about the need for exercise—both physical and mental—and general education about the effect of attention—both positive and negative—I addressed the problem.

As tempting as it may be to respond to the owner's concern about an individual behavior, it is unfair and ineffective to try to resolve it outside of the context of the dog's whole life. Behaviors do not simply spring out of thin air; they start for a reason. Understand that reason and you can control that behavior.

By redirecting Duncan with obedience instead of chasing him around, adding in a healthy dose of daily romping, leaving a lead on him when they were home so they could calmly get immediate control, and refocusing him on more positive behaviors, they were able to get him to stop this unwanted, if amusing, canine behavior quite quickly. The human behavior took a little longer. They continued to walk up the stairs sideways, glancing over their shoulders, for several weeks after Duncan had given up the chase.

Dog Day Afternoon (SARAH)

If you ever want to see true breed temperament on full display, go to an agility event. In agility, dogs work off lead, climbing over, scrambling through, weaving in and out, and generally having a marvelous time completing an obstacle course.

I had the pleasure of announcing an event for a humane society fund-raising dinner one year. Because it was for exhibition only, this was a nice place for less competitive club members to have fun with their dogs.

My favorite performance was given by an older red Chow named Ming. Chows are not generally built for speed or athleticism, and Ming was no exception. Jeanne, her twenty-something owner, must have been a cheerleader in high school.

"Come on, Ming! Are you ready? That's a good girl!" Jeanne called out, clapping her hands and crouching in the position of a relay racer about to get handed the baton.

Ming sat at the starting line, her head turned to the side, contemplating the husky behind her.

"Go!" the timer called out.

"Come on, Ming!" Jeanne shouted as she bolted toward the first set of jumps.

Ming watched Jeanne go. After a moment or two of thought, Ming heaved her weight forward over her front end and rose onto all fours. She then ambled in Jeanne's general direction.

Standing next to the first low jump, Jeanne called out encouragement. "Jump! Ming, good girl, what a dog!" Ming trotted up to the jump and stopped, gazing off toward the buffet table.

Bending over, clapping her hands wildly, Jeanne tapped the jump. "Jump! Atta girl, you're doing great!" Ming wagged her tail once. For those of you who doubt that a dog can make a single wag, then stop, I suggest you watch a Chow who adores her owner but abhors an activity.

Suddenly, without warning, Ming popped over the jump in rocking horse style. Having proved to all that she could do it if she wanted, she trotted around the next two jumps in the line.

This display instilled new determination in her owner. "All right! Good job! Come on!" Jeanne called out as she raced to the tunnel. There she clapped wildly as Ming followed at a slow trot. The tunnel involved no physical effort for her of any kind beyond ducking her head, so she entered it without pausing.

Jeanne ran to the next obstacle, the A-frame, which is a climbing obstacle that looks like two doors leaning against each other. There is always a chain or bar securing the doors to each other halfway down, giving the whole thing the appearance of a large A.

With Ming out of sight, Jeanne stopped cheering. Without Jeanne's cheering, the bumping in the tunnel that accompanied the dog's progress stopped. Seconds ticked by—no Ming. As the crowd fell silent in anticipation, Jeanne raced back to the tunnel. Dropping to her knees, she peered into the opening. "Come on, Ming! Good girl!" The bumping resumed. Ming exited the tunnel only to pause as she considered the crowd for a few moments. Whether this was a stress reaction on her part, or a form of mental resistance, or simply something she had developed to drive Jeanne into heightened levels of cheering, I cannot say. But it was classic, and the crowd roared with laughter.

BRIAN KILCOMMONS / SARAH WILSON

Eventually, Ming completed the course in her own way. She politely declined the A-frame, the see-saw, and the weave poles. At the finish line, while a panting Jeanne hugged her, Ming wagged her tail once, then looked off into the distance with just the faintest hint of a Chowish grin on her face.

MAYBE IT'S NOT THE DOG

Sorry We Missed It (SARAH)

As we were standing around at the entry table at a local Australian Shepherd show, a woman came up wringing her hands. "Do you have Novice A?" she asked in a high-pitched voice. Novice is the first level of competition obedience and the A class is for any owner who has never before obtained an obedience degree. Without waiting a second, she repeated, "Do you have Novice A?"

Trying to calm her a bit, I smiled and replied, "Yes, there is Novice A here, but there is also Pre Novice, if you're not quite ready. . . ."

"Oh, no, we've trained; we've practiced," she said with confidence as she grabbed an entry form and filled it out.

I shrugged to myself. When you're that nervous, better to start off at an easy level until you get your head together, but it's America and you can do what you want.

I soon forgot all about her. As the show got under way, I parked myself by the obedience rings to watch. It's always interesting. At my first dog show, at the age of ten or so, I discovered obedience. I sat by the ring, glued to the proceedings for four hours while my mother desperately had me paged over the loudspeaker. When I finally snapped out of my dog-induced trance, I heard the tired voice of the announcer saying, "Paging Sarah Wilson, lost but not forgotten."

I enjoy watching and occasionally I compete. Competition is not my best suit. I was not born loving precision, which this sport calls for in spades. Still, I enjoy it.

Anyway, I was parked at ringside when the woman entered the ring. She had a nice young dark blue merle male Australian Shepherd with her who looked mighty energetic from my vantage point. The first exercise was heeling on lead. This means that the dog walks next to the owner's left side, close but not touching, paying strict attention to every move the owner makes. When done properly, it is a dance between two species.

She took her position and told her dog, Dillinger, to sit. He looked off into the distance. She repeated herself. He showed no sign of hearing her. She shoved his butt down hard into a sit. Rough handling of any kind is a big no-no in the ring.

I glanced at the woman next to me; our eyes met, widening slightly. This was not a promising start. The judge asked if she was ready. She shifted on her feet, then nodded yes. "Dillinger, Heel," she said loudly, swinging her left leg out in her first stride. As the leg passed his head, the dog grabbed it. With her pant leg firmly in his jaws, he threw his weight backward, beginning a wild game of tug-of-war.

There was a collective gasp from the observers. This

would be similar to a concert pianist striding on stage, sitting down, then banging on the keyboard senselessly.

Keeping her eyes forward, the woman used her lead to pull him off. This urged him on to heightened levels of rambunctiousness. In this manner, they proceeded through the entire exercise, she making every effort to keep him off her and he walking sideways, lunging madly at her pant leg. Many of us were stifling laughter. A crowd of people gathered to watch this debacle.

The rest of the exercises were in the same horrific vein. The last individual Novice exercise is the off-lead heel. Even the stone-faced judge showed a bit of concern when he asked if she was ready. "Ready," the owner said surprisingly merrily. As her left leg swung out for the first stride, Dillinger grabbed the cuff. Swinging his weight back over his haunches, he pulled with all his might. Momentarily stopped, she leaned into the task and continued down the ring, dragging the growling dog behind her. He shook his head, which in turn shook her leg wildly. He tugged rhythmically, in an effort to make her heed him. She never looked down. She did the whole exercise, walking the complete length of the ring, making the turns, doing the halts and restarts, dragging this Tasmanian devil behind her.

At this point, we all felt serious pity, group support for a novice, and comic disbelief. I've been to a lot of shows and watched many, many bad performances, even given a few myself, but never have I witnessed anything like this.

As the woman left the ring, tears streamed from her eyes.

Several of us flocked to her, offering words of comfort. "He'll improve with some work. Everyone has bad days."

"No, no," she said, waving one hand at us, shaking her head, snorting slightly as she tried to catch her breath. "You don't understand. He was so much better than last time." She walked off, weeping in happiness.

Love You, But . . . (SARAH)

In 1986, I almost managed to kill myself. Not intentionally, mind you, just a bad combination of a high pain tolerance, ridiculous medical advice, and an unwillingness to inconvenience anyone at 2:00 A.M.

What I did was rupture my appendix. That sounds painful, you say. Yes, it was. But I had never had food poisoning before, so I chalked the cramping up to some flounder I'd had for dinner that night.

After the appendix ruptured, the pain lessened greatly, so I just stayed in bed. A home-visit doctor stopped by. He did the classic test for appendicitis, and when I screamed, he said, "If you don't feel better in a couple of days, go see a real doctor."

The doctor did manage to help me out, though. He told me to eat. When I ate, the pain took on a proportion that I hadn't known existed. Suddenly, I understood buckling under torture. When I finally got to Lenox Hill's emergency room and the doctor was examining my gangrenous, peritonitis-filled abdomen, I would have sold my soul to the devil to stop him.

I screamed so loudly, he told me I was making him feel bad. I stopped long enough to explain to him that his feelings were not my responsibility and that if he was going to make a living probing infected places, he had better expect it.

The rest of this story is entertaining, especially since I lived to tell it, but it doesn't have much to do with dogs, so I'll skip to the dog part. I'll fill you in on the rest some other time. Anyway, a couple of surgeries later I came home after a month in the hospital. I was eager to return to my regular life. One of the first things I did was some training with Kesl, my Bouvier, down in our basement. Nothing big. It just felt good to be working with a dog.

Since I was not up to handling a lead yet, I decided to work on directional retrieving. That's where you lay out a number of objects, usually three, and use a hand signal as well as a voice command to tell the dog which one you want him to pick up. It's a relatively quiet exercise—no turns, little walking—and I could go at my own speed. What I didn't take into account was my mental condition, which was, frankly, not so good. General anesthesia can really take it out of you. Two generals, both of which had me under for several hours, losing over twenty-five pounds, and the physical stress of the medication, fear, pain, and having my insides shoved around left me not quite myself.

Kesl was more than willing to work. He was happy to see me, having missed training himself, I think. In the first round of retrieving, I pointed at the glove on the right and said, "Take it!" In the next setup, I said, "Left," which was not only a different command altogether but simply wrong. My dyslexia was acute at that stage of recovery. On the third attempt, I gave a different command, which I can't recall, but I do remember Kesl's reaction.

After I gave the signal and the command, Kess sat next to me, staring up at my face. Looking at me from under those bushy black eyebrows, he inhaled deeply. Slowly, he let the air escape in a mammoth sigh; then he got up and walked out of the room. I heard him drop onto a mattress we had in the next room. Bouviers do not so much lie down as simply lift up all four paws and tumble earthward. It sounds something like a bureau tipping over, which can scare the heck out of you late at night in an empty house if you don't know they do that.

I stood staring after him for a moment; then I laughed as much as my incisions would allow. He was right, as he almost always was. It was too soon. I was no one worth following yet, which he had just pointed out in such a kind, dignified manner. Taking his suggestion, I joined him on the mattress for a nap. That worked out fine for both of us.

You're Scared, Remember! (BRIAN)

Dog owners, and parents, have to keep up with their charges, and I don't mean just physically. A friend took her large German Shepherd, Quincy, to a pet-supply store to pick out a new dog toy. As she turned down one aisle, a woman exclaimed, "Oh, my son is terrified of big dogs. Absolutely terrified," she repeated, glancing around. My friend gathered that her son was somewhere in the store. "Well, then, this is a wonderful dog for him to meet," my friend responded. "He's very gentle." "Oh, no." The woman shook her head, again hurriedly glancing around. "He'll be so frightened."

My friend smiled and walked on. Odd place to bring a child if he is frightened of dogs, she thought to herself. As she and Quincy rounded the next corner, they ran smack into the child and his father. The little boy turned, his mouth an O of surprise. For a moment, my friend thought he might scream or run, but instead he exclaimed, "What a big dog!" and ran over to Quincy. Beaming, he proudly petted the big dog's gleaming coat. Quincy's mouth hung open, tongue lolling in a silly, relaxed canine grin.

Just then, his mother appeared. She froze in place. "But you're terrified of dogs, honey." Hurrying to him, she grabbed his arm, pulling him away. Bending over, she looked him square in the face. "You hate big dogs. You're frightened of them, remember?" The child's face was blank with confusion. "Remember?" she said again, giving his arm a shake.

Her husband scowled: He was not amused when his son broke down in tears. As the father moved toward the boy, my friend and her canine ambassador turned away. This was clearly a family matter. Shaking her head slowly, she looked down at Quincy. "Not your fault, Quinn, you were great." Scratching his huge skull, she went to buy yet another sacrificial stuffed toy hedgehog.

Why We Make the Big Bucks (SARAH)

Brian did not want me to take the Browns' dog, Muffin, in for boarding. Muffin wasn't the problem; it was the Browns. Anyone who asks Brian to brush their dog's teeth with two different toothbrushes is in for a rough road. I, however, found the Browns devoted to, if a bit overboard about, their dog. This is not especially unusual in our work, so I booked their dog for the week.

Muffin, an older Shepherd mix, arrived at our home with a veritable vanload of survival gear. Along with five meals a day, each in its own labeled plastic container, numerous toys, a special blanket, medical supplies, graham crackers, flashlights, Q-Tips, cotton balls, and more, we got the following set of typed instructions for her care. We offer it to you, we swear, exactly as it was handed to us.

"Muffin is fed five times per day, at 7:00 A.M., 10:30 A.M., 1:30 P.M., 5:30 P.M., and 9:00 P.M. The prepared servings are labeled for the corresponding meals. They should be heated to room temperature to take off the chill. (If she is licking her chops and looks like she is bringing something up in her throat, feed her the 10:30 A.M. feeding early, but no earlier than 10:00 A.M. If this happens, she can be fed the 1:30 meal at 1:15 but no earlier, only if necessary—she will let you know.) Please do not mix up the times of the labeled meals, because some contain vitamins she can only tolerate at certain times of the day.

"She should have a generous dollop of chicken soup with meals, heated to room temperature to take off the chill and blended in with the rest of her meal to smooth out the food into a creamy, pudding consistency. Water should be at room temperature, unless it is extremely hot outside; then it can be cool.

"She can have a slice of roast beef torn into bite sizes as a snack. It should also be heated to room temperature.

"She gets brewer's yeast pills two times per day, at 10:30 A.M. and at 5:30 P.M. She gets three pills each time. Tell her to 'chew, chew, chew.' (Yes, we do say it three times; otherwise, she will swallow it whole.) Give her one pill at a time, not all three at once. She knows brewer's yeast as 'b y's.'

"If she gets sick, it will usually be between 5:00 A.M. and 6:30 A.M. If this happens, she will regurgitate bile, usually between one and three mouthfuls. After this happens, she may look guilty, as if she has done something wrong. We reassure her that she did not. Tell her she is a good girl (lots of positive reinforcement). We give her a tablespoon of Coca-Cola syrup, which normally settles her stomach. This is not an incident that would require veterinary care. Take her outside immediately and let her run it off. If she gets sick more than the once in the morning, and it is accompanied by diarrhea, phone us immediately. You can usually tell if she is going to get sick. She gets a 'look' in her eyes. Her eyes are usually bright, sparkly, and clear. If sick, she gets a cloudy cast look in her eyes.

"Okay. Now, believe it or not . . . If you are having a hard time getting her to go out, tell her to go '*o u t*'—she understands the spelling and will listen.

"When you take her out, tell her to 'go make doody'; she usually will. She needs to go out first thing in the morning, before she is fed. Do not leave her unsupervised in areas where there is dog stool or grass. She will eat it. Frequent trips outside in the morning (two to three times) will probably alleviate any problems. She will have two bowel movements per day. If she gets runny, mix in 1/4 teaspoon only of Tylan powder daily in her food. Let her go out after meals.

"At bedtime, Muffin gets two graham crackers (one sheet).

"If there are thunderstorms, she becomes extremely frightened. Letting her lie down on the bathroom rug we brought will usually calm her down. Tell her to lie down on Magic Carpet. It helps greatly to close any venetian blinds in the room, put on an air conditioner, and turn the volume of the TV or radio up to drown out the thunder. If she could stay with someone, it would comfort her.

"Important—her nicknames are Muffy, Bubba Angel Bear, Boo Boo Baby Bear, Fin-fin (for Sarah—Mommy's Little Baby), Kabooba Baby Bear, or any combination of the above. Anything with a Baby in it. She likes 'Where's Mommy's Little . . .' preceding it. She likes her tush and hind legs rubbed. If necessary, brush and comb her.

"On Sunday, her ears should be cleaned and dried using a cotton swab saturated with Oti-Clens to clean and cotton balls to dry. We put a flashlight in for your use. Then put a dab of ointment in each ear, one at a time, and massage gently. Also, please put her blanket in her cage with her.

"On Saturday night and Monday night, if possible, Muffin's teeth need to be brushed. Please use both brushes.

"Her favorite toy is the pacifier (She knows it as 'Binky'). She also knows Booda rope ('Booda'), Tweety Bird, sterilized bones (Kerchunkle bone—because when she drops it, it makes a *kerchunk* noise), Dino bone. Frisbee is her favorite outdoor toy. If someone could play Frisbee with her, she would really enjoy it.

"This may seem like a lot of work, but it really isn't. The day goes by very quickly and is usually uneventful. We do not call her a dog—she is a 'puppy person.' In addition, she is not spoiled, only well maintained.

"She is sensitive and needs lots of positive reinforcement and TLC. She likes to be told she is a good girl and is wonderful. She is extremely well behaved and you will find she is very little trouble. She is very affectionate and likes to give lots of kisses, especially on the face. She gets along well with other dogs.

"Yes, you must return her to us after the weekend."

As an addendum, during her stay with us, Muffin showed no response to her name, praise, or any of the words in her expansive vocabulary. She slept most of the time, exhibiting zero stress or anxiety, regardless of the noise level. She showed every sign of being a normal, if supremely phlegmatic, dog.

Finding Rocky (SARAH)

The thing that stood in the middle of the dirt road, blocking my van, looked like something from the Middle Ages—a cross perhaps between a bear and a werewolf. Five-inch-long black hair stuck out from his head in all directions; his legs, like black columns, were full of leaves; his back was nearly hairless. I was probably one of five people in a twenty-mile radius who would have known what he was—a raggedy Bouvier des Flandres. But what was he doing on the edge of a 3,500-acre park, clearly having been on his own for a while?

This was years after Kesl, but I still knew a Bouv when I saw one. Pulling the van over, I turned off the engine, staring in some amazement. This dog faced me in front of an abandoned old house with boarded-up windows. He was not moving, not threatening, not frightened. He just stood looking at me—typical Bouv.

As usual, I had a box of biscuits and a lead in the car. Grabbing both, I stepped out into the road. I extended my hand, offering him something to eat. He did not move. I tossed a biscuit in front of him. He looked at me, then reached down carefully and picked up my offering. As he ate, I approached him, talking all the way. He stood his ground. When I got within about six feet, I stopped. He'd have to come the rest of the way if he wanted my help. I squatted down, offering another biscuit. Slowly, he came forward. As he reached out delicately to take the food, I got a good look at the mess of tangles that was his beard and a good whiff of his stench. Bearded dogs can have a wet beard odor even with excellent care. Without care, they stink. He stank.

I reached up and scratched the matted fur on his chest. He accepted this. Talking to him calmly, I clipped the lead onto the worn, grubby red collar he wore. Chatting some more, I quickly ran my hand underneath him, checking for swollen teats. I didn't want to leave any pups stranded. That's when I discovered he was a he, in all his glory.

He was skinny, bald on top, but, external appearance to the contrary, he seemed to be a nice dog. We walked to the van together; he did not pull. Sliding the door open, I encouraged him in. Without hesitation, he hopped on up, standing behind the driver's seat. I tethered the lead so he could not wander, but I doubted it would be a problem. With another couple of biscuits for the road, he and I went home.

He turned out to be a lovely dog—a lovely dog whom no one ever claimed, even though we advertised thoroughly and called every shelter and dog-control officer in the area. One woman said someone had lost a Bouvier over a year ago. I tried to track her down, but she had moved. I had no success. Could this dog have been on his own for a year? His appearance certainly pointed to that possibility. Why would he have come out of hiding now? Why would he have chosen me to reveal himself to? Whether it was ESP, good luck, or fate, not many people would have stopped for this dog. He looked like a nightmare come to life standing on that isolated road in the woods.

Turns out he had mange, a painful ear infection, as well as a bellyful of parasites. We got all that taken care of and had him neutered to boot. Once we knew he was healthy and just as nice as we had initially thought he was, we called Bouvier Rescue. They got him placed in a loving home with a couple of kids. The day his new family came to pick him up, he took a shine to them instantly, especially the kids.

After greeting them in the front yard, he pulled me to their van, hopping in on his own. He lay down in front of the youngest's car seat and refused to get out. His decision was final. His new family couldn't have been more pleased.

Love Makes You Do Funny Things (BRIAN)

Celeste had no use for dogs. Worse than that, she hated the Maltese who lived with her new husband, William. Sprite, the Maltese, was a nice-enough little dog who had a leg-lifting problem. Actually, Sprite didn't consider it a problem—he enjoyed lifting his leg—but it was a problem for Celeste.

Celeste and William's town house on the East Side looked like a textbook on antiques, especially the third-floor formal sitting room. Naturally, Sprite had a particular fascination with watering furniture on the third floor. This outraged Celeste.

We went over all the training needed, but frankly, she just didn't like the dog much. With William off on business a great deal, Sprite ended up confined most of the time. He stayed in the kitchen with the housekeeper, unless there was a lot of traffic through that room; then he was parked in the dumbwaiter, with the door open. He never jumped down; it worked like an open-air crate.

Celeste's dislike for Sprite grew over the months. She found him dirty, refusing to change his papers when he left his tiny Tootsie Roll poops on them. *Repulsive*, I believe, was the word she used.

Finally, for the sake of all concerned, we placed Sprite in a loving home, where he is, even as I write this, cherished. This happy, expansive Queens family are constantly astounded that he responds to simple commands and does a few tricks. This gives them no end of pleasure. Their house, being smaller than Celeste and William's, with a readily accessible backyard, made getting control of his leg lifting easier. Not that they mind it much. It just doesn't bother them when he occasionally douses the corner of the couch. A happy ending for Sprite. Sometimes, people and dogs just don't match. Celeste and Sprite certainly did not.

We thought that was the end of it, dogwise, for this couple, but a few months later Celeste contacted us. "Can you find me a really big dog?" Celeste must have heard my eyebrows shoot up over the phone. "William wants a big dog more than anything and I want to give him the dog as a gift. He wants an Irish Wolfhound. Is that right?" I pointed out the resolution to the problem of her last canine companion.

"I know, I know," she agreed over the phone, "but William hardly ever wants anything, and he wants this." There was a long pause, then rather softly, she said, "I want to give him this." I could tell from her tone that she was sincere.

Sarah and I had major reservations about this whole situation. I had several serious discussions with Celeste about this plan. I explained the realities and the responsibilities of having a dog this large. Celeste had all the right answers. After much soul-searching, Sarah and I decided to help her. She was clearly committed to the project and we did not want her heading off to a pet store. Privately, we both wondered how Celeste would cope. She said she was ready. We hoped she was right.

After some checking around, we located a five-month-old male who sounded perfect—out of good lines, mellow, and sweet. I drove five hours into Pennsylvania to pick him up from the breeder. The youngster was everything the breeder said he would be.

Celeste and William arrived for the great meeting. They sat together, holding hands, on the tan leather couch against the wall. William leaned forward, positively glowing with anticipation. Celeste sat next to him, watching his every expression with obvious pleasure. Sarah stood by, ready to help with any awkward moments during the introduction. We both had visions of the pup leaping on Celeste, snagging her sweater with a claw or in some other way upsetting this woman. I walked the pup into the room. As expected, William's smile reached from ear to ear. His eyes filled with delight as he stared at this wonderful dog. "Oh, he's so beautiful!" he exclaimed gleefully.

But the pup didn't hear him. The dog and Celeste were locked in some cosmic moment. No one in the room existed for that Wolfhound but Celeste and no one in the room existed for Celeste but that dog. The big-pawed pup flopped his way over to her, burying his head in her lap. She stroked him almost reverently. "Oh, William," Celeste said, turning to her husband. "Oh, he's so sweet." William's face was a portrait of mixed emotions. Clearly, he was thrilled his wife was happy—he was, like all of us, completely taken aback—yet for a second, a glimmer of disappointment flashed across his kind face because the dog hadn't gone to him.

As Celeste tells it, Goliath, as she named the pup, is her reward for being willing to sacrifice her wants for her husband's. She says that, in her moment of spiritual generosity, God rewarded her with this special being.

She could be right. Who else but God could have rendered such a change? Now this born-again dog lover is a fanatic. Celeste, "Miss I Won't Touch Sprite's Dirty Papers," bends down behind a mature Wolfhound, holding the newspaper under him as he's making a deposit that would probably outweigh Sprite himself.

"I'd catch it in my hands if I had to," she says. "It's not disgusting. It's Goliath's."

Dumped by My Dog (SARAH)

There is an old saying that if you love something, let it go. If it returns to you, it is yours forever. If it does not, it never was yours to begin with. Apparently, Kesl was never mine, but for six years I thought he was.

Kesl had been purchased from an ad in the *New York Times*. My then husband, Peter, was not thrilled with my idea of a Doberman, and I wasn't much in love with his idea of an Old English Sheepdog. We compromised on a Bouvier, which had the hairy look he wanted and the protectiveness I wanted.

We were without a car at that point in our lives, so the woman who bred the litter brought all nine pups in for us to look at. I carefully puppy-tested each in the hall outside of our apartment door. Several were okay, one was a great combination, being intelligent, calm, and stable, and one was a screamer. We selected the calm, stable one. After money exchanged hands and the breeder left, our pup started to howl. Upon examination, we realized we had picked up the screamer by mistake. Or maybe the woman had pulled a fast one. She never did return our phone calls or letters regarding Kesl's progress.

In any case, though we had some trying months of noisy puppyhood, with training, Kesl grew into a wonderful dog.

We did pet therapy work together, visiting nursing homes and schools. We earned a C.D., the basic-level AKC obedience degree, in three consecutive shows. He protected me more than once when I didn't know I was in danger, and he ignored me completely twice when I thought I was. We were inseparable.

When Brian and I started our training business in Manhattan, our lives changed. We worked fifteen to seventeen hours a day, seven days a week. I trained everyone else's dog but my own. Kesl, not a demanding dog, took to sleeping in the corner and sighing a lot. I knew he missed my time with him. I knew he hated to share me with one other dog, never mind dozens. I gave him my attention when I could, but he was not happy with the arrangement, and I could hardly blame him.

Many months into this life, a friend's world crumbled. Andie's mother died, just a few years after her father had passed away. She was not close to her one sibling and she battled with a demon I knew all too well, an eating disorder.

I called regularly but did not like what I heard. No, she hadn't gotten dressed today. No, she hadn't gone outside all week. No, she wasn't eating well. This was not good, not good at all. I tried to talk to her. I got short answers, in a monotone voice, She was on a downhill slope. What could I do to help?

Then I had a thought. Andie adored my dogs, especially Kesl, whom she often took for long walks on the weekends when our training center was particularly busy. Maybe he could help where I could not. I picked up the phone.

"Andie, I hate to ask, but I could use a favor," I said nonchalantly. "Things are crazy here. Kess is bored; he could use some special attention. I hate to ask, but I wondered if you might . . ." I let my voice trail off. She agreed to help. So off my boy went to the biggest pet therapy task of his life.

Immediately, the phone calls got better. Andie sounded almost lively. Kesl slept on her bed, keeping night demons away. She started eating more so she could give him treats from her plate. During his walks, people stopped her to ask about him. She chatted. He lay at her feet. She felt safe. He looked in her eyes. She felt loved. After a few days, I went to visit, to check on my dog. I knocked at the door. I heard his bear paws just on the other side. She spoke to him briefly before she opened the door. As the door swung open, he bounced excitedly. Visitors, visitors! Then he saw who it was. He stopped bouncing, looked at me, and turned away.

From that moment on and until the last time I saw him, Kesl would not give me the time of day. I could walk him, pet him, do whatever, but he never acknowledged me as anything but a supremely uninteresting stranger.

As I sat in her living room, looking at them together, her hand resting casually, lovingly on his bulky shoulders, he lying in bliss on the couch next to her, head resting on her thighs, I knew asking for him back was wrong.

I could not say to her, "Listen, now that you have attached to another living thing, now that you have loved again and found some semblance of safety, give him back. He's mine."

I could not say to him, "Now that you have found some-one who needs you, has time for you, dotes on you, and whom you clearly adore, come back with me because I own you."

I let him go, not because I wanted to, but because it was the right thing to do, for both of them—which is the noble reason. The not-so-noble reason is that he wasn't mine any-more anyway. I couldn't stand looking at my dog lying in the corner of our office sighing, dreaming of another per-son and another life. He had made his choice. I honored that choice.

So they stayed together. Andie called me once or twice a year, often in tears, saying how much she loved that big hairy beast. I could not have been prouder of him.

A FOOTNOTE:

I just spoke to Andie, who sobbed on the phone that Kesl, at twelve and a half, has liver cancer. She wanted to know when it would be time to put him to sleep. Barely able to speak the words, she asked me, "What if I do it too soon? I don't want to do it too soon." The sentence faded into tears. "But," she added, "I couldn't stand it if he suffered. He can't suffer." Again, the phone line filled with grief.

There are no easy answers. None of us has a crystal ball. Being able to take our animal companion's life to stop re-lentless suffering is a great gift and a terrible curse.

During this phone call, she shared a story with me. We were talking about how much Kesl connected to her and how important they were to each other.

"One day, I was on the bed reading, and he laid his head on my stomach, resting its full weight there, which is pretty heavy. Putting the book aside, I stroked his head. 'Kesl, I'm going to tell you a story. Once there was a Bouvier named Kesl. And he came to visit Andie. And Andie loved Kesl and Kesl loved Andie. Then one day, an envelope came in the mail.' At that point, Kesl lifted his head and started to lick my face. 'I know,' I told him, 'this is my favorite part, too. And in it was a dog tag and his papers and a note. And I knew then that Kesl was going to be with Andie forever.' And Kesl put his head back on my lap with a sigh of contentment." She did not speak for several seconds.

"It's like he knew," she told me, her voice cracking under the strain. "He knew exactly what I was saying."

"Of course he did," I told her. "He's your Kesl."

Give the Dog a Break (BRIAN)

Shnooky's owner, Susan, was not an especially happy woman. Although extremely successful in her career selling cars and wealthy because of it, she seemed to lack emotional richness in the rest of her life, which made her look to her Shepherd mix for some fulfillment.

Some of my all-time favorite phone calls have come from this devoted, if frequently misguided, owner. Here are a couple of examples:

"Hello, Brian?"

"Hi, Susan, what's up?"

"I'm worried about my little Shnookums."

BRIAN KILCOMMONS / SARAH WILSON

"Oh, nothing serious, I hope?"

"Well, I don't know. I walk her twice a day and Justine, my new housekeeper, walks her three times when I'm gone, but Shnookum's having only three bowel movements a day."

"That sounds perfectly normal."

"It is? Are you sure? I have more than three a day. Shouldn't she have at least as many as I am having? Couldn't she be constipated? What if she's uncomfortable? Can I add bran to her food? Do you think she needs an enema?"

"Whoa, whoa, Susan. Don't do anything! Do you hear me? Three is normal; two would be normal. If she is otherwise healthy—energy fine, attitude fine, appetite fine—don't fix what isn't broken."

"Ohhhh—" Susan moaned.

"Listen," I cut in, "if you're worried, call your vet, okay?"

"Dr. Rosa!" I could hear her voice perk up. "Good idea, I'll check with him. . . ."

It was a wonder Shnooky was as normal as she was, all things considered. Susan is the type of woman who calls professionals until she finds one who, from belief or just being worn down, agrees with her.

Another call came July seventh or so.

"Brian? I'm so worried. Shnooky won't come out from under my bed."

"When did this start? Was the Fourth hard for her?" I knew Shnooky was sensitive to noise.

"It was terrible. She hid, trembling. I was so worried. I told her not to be silly. I even carried her outside to show her what the big bangs were."

"You carried her outside during the fireworks?"

"Oh yes. I pointed to the sky, but she wouldn't look up. I thought if she could just see them, she wouldn't be so scared."

Just my luck. A client who refuses to force her dog to do anything decides to change her stripes on one of the most traumatic days of the year for a sound-sensitive dog. I was surprised Shnooky hadn't bitten Susan in her panic.

As far as I know, Shnooky is still under the bed, and Susan is still calling people, hoping for the answers she wants to hear.

What Goes In (SARAH)

A black-and-white French Bulldog, Tyke, graced one of my classes. I have always admired this charming blunt-faced breed, though their snorting and gas-passing habits will deter me from ever having one myself.

They are comical little dogs, and Tyke was no exception. He did, however, have a problem. His distraught owners had taken him to several vets and a few specialists to determine the cause of his chronically loose stool. Nobody could find anything wrong. It was a mystery.

During class one day, Tyke got caught short and relieved himself on the floor. I knew immediately what the problem was.

"Ah, Gerald?" I asked the owner innocently. "Exactly how much are you feeding Tyke?"

Gerald thought for a moment. "About five cups," he said.

"A day!?" I wanted to be sure I'd understood him properly.

"Yes, a day." He nodded his head.

"Let's do a little math. It's not exactly the same, but you'll get the idea. Tyke weighs twenty pounds and you are giving him five cups. How much do you weigh?"

Gerald answered, "About one eighty."

"Okay, so you are nine times as big as Tyke. What would happen if you ate forty-five cups of food a day?"

"Forty-five!" He looked at Tyke.

"Right," I said. "He needs something like two cups a day. Betcha he'll be normal in no time."

And he was. A wise vet once told me, "When you hear hoofbeats in the night, think horse, not zebra." Sometimes the most obvious things are the hardest to see.

DISASTER DU JOUR

Get My Drift? (SARAH)

There are many patterns to Brian's and my life together, but one die-hard rule is that any major storm inevitably will hit when he is out of town. The winter storm of '93 was no exception. We had thirteen storms worth talking about that year in Middletown, New York; the one this story is about was *the* storm of that winter.

I can't tell you precisely how many inches fell that day and into the night. I didn't have time to mess around with a measuring stick. This complaining is coming from a true winter person. If you put a gun to my head and made me choose Florida or Alaska, it would be no contest. Pack my bags, I'm going north.

Of course, the kennel was full that week. The storm started late in the afternoon. It was a fierce nor'easter, full of whipping winds, snow that hit you like a sandblaster, bitter cold. I put off running the dogs for as long as possible, hoping the storm would abate a bit. It strengthened. The poor dogs had to go out. I donned two layers of socks, my snowmobile boots, my insulated zip-up coveralls, two heavy scarves wrapped in opposite directions, and a hat pulled down low. The Pillsbury Doughboy shows more shape than I do in that outfit. But, with the exception of my eyes, no amount of cold bothers me, so fashion be damned.

The door in the kennel that leads to the runs opens it. It

needed a hefty pull to get it unfrozen. The drift that had been pressed against the door looked as if it had been sliced with a knife. It was over my knees. The light over the door, which normally illuminates the whole back area, cast only a small circle of light. It, too, was hemmed in by the storm.

I shoveled my way out to the first pen, shoveled it open, shoveled some of the highest-drifting snow over the fence—didn't want anyone walking out of our runs, which was rapidly becoming a danger.

The wind was wild. By the time I had shoveled the back of the run a bit, I had to remove several inches away from the gate just to reopen it to get out. Snow was moving like water. I went in to get a Golden Retriever out of his kennel.

Out in the snow, he romped in the drifts, burying his face, only to pull it up, sugar-coated, to sneeze. At least one of us was having fun. Reshoveling the gate free, I put him in the run. While he did his business, I attacked the next run. I knew if I waited till morning, the gates could freeze in place, and then I'd be in real trouble.

In I went to get the next dog. Out I came, only to have to reshovel what I had just done. Getting the Golden out required more demolition. Then in he came. I pulled the snowballs out from between his toes, brushed off the icicles from his belly, tossed a dry mat into his crate, and put him to bed for the night.

Shedding clothing as the sweat started, out I went again. Somewhere between the fifth and sixth excursion, the lights went out. Blessedly, some of the dogs could be run in groups. Several simply stood by the gate, looking pathetic when I shut it. I knew the feeling, but this wouldn't do. They had to relieve themselves or they'd have me up in a few hours, complaining about their full bladders. The thought of leaving a warm, cozy bed to face this wintry onslaught did not appeal to me. They had to go.

So I went in to play with them. A romp would help them relax and a relaxed dog goes to the bathroom, and a dog who has done that sleeps through the night.

Tossing snowballs for dogs who leap up, catch the crumbling toy in their mouths, or dive headfirst after it, is exhilarating even in the dark, in a storm, when the electricity is out. I chased them around. They spun in glee, the smaller ones leaping through the white like furry dolphins, their barking muffled by the storm. We all ran until we were breathless. Panting, I shoveled us free from the newly drifted snow. Inside, the dogs clicked across the linoleum on feet like icy castanets.

Standing for a minute, breathing hard, listening to the dogs mill about the kennel, smelling the warm, wet dog smell, I leaned against the doorjamb. All were safe. All were cared for. I relaxed for a second.

Then nasty little gnawing thoughts entered my mind. How long would the electricity be out? Would the dogs be warm enough? Could I take them all upstairs if need be?

I could. It would mean hauling some crates upstairs, but okay. It was possible. If we were all in one room, we'd be warm. After all, normal canine body temperature is 101.5°. That's downright toasty. Secure that I had a plan if it came to that, I got back to work.

Finally, all my charges were bedded down. Each had warm blankets and a bone to chew on. I left them all snug in their beds to start the upstairs projects. Since they had relieved themselves, I had a shot at getting some sleep. I also had a tiny bit of flexibility in the morning if I had to wrestle with frozen kennel latches before I could get them outside.

Now, I had other concerns. Our little home was a bit in the boondocks. I was not sure how long it would take to get power restored. If the break was local, no one might be able to get to our dirt road for days. Exhausted, sweaty, and more than a little overwhelmed, I contemplated my next moves. First, hang blankets over the five-by-eight picture window in the living room. Up they went with duct tape, in candlelight.

Then I wrapped the refrigerator in another not-so-old blanket. I'm not sure that L. L. Bean had this use in mind when they made their thick wool blankets. Taping a blanket in place around a refrigerator isn't the simplest thing to do by yourself. I managed, but not without considerable cursing.

After that, I tucked towels in place at the bottoms of the doors to keep in even more heat. Then I flopped into a chair to call my dear friends down the road, who knew all about emergencies such as this. A serious discussion followed about how to drain the water pipes. Hanging up, I sighed, made myself a cup of tea with some of the last hot water left in the water dispenser we had in the kitchen, and called Brian at his hotel in Arizona. The phone rang in his room. No answer. "Would you like to leave a message?" asked the dutifully bubbly hotel operator.

"No thank you," I replied grumpily. What was I going

to say? "Why aren't you home?" or "I hate that you are away in the sun"?

Gathering my wits, I headed down to the basement. With detailed notes from my conversation with my neighbor clutched in my hand, I stood staring at all the pipes I had never much noticed before. Main valve? Somewhere in here a main valve was hidden? Then the phone rang.

"Hey, honey. How's it going?" came Brian's cheerful voice.

"Where have you been? I've been trying to reach you." Not cheerful.

"Oh, down at the pool. You know, this place has a great Jacuzzi. It's really nice. They have a solarium built off the pool area. . . ." He sounded so relaxed and happy.

"How nice for you," I replied sarcastically as I hung up on him.

I didn't want to hear about his wonderful day, about him soaking luxuriously in a warm tub. To be totally honest, I wanted him to be miserable, too. How dare he be happy—comfortable—carefree.

After a few moments of sorting out my motives, I called him back to apologize. He accepted it with good humor. After our call, I went to bed, setting my clock for 3:00 A.M. I'd check the heat in the house then, drain pipes if I needed to, and move dogs if necessary. Right now, I needed some sleep. The lights coming on woke me at two or so. The storm passed, as they always do. The sun came up onto that sparkling perfection that is a poststorm landscape before anything walks across it.

Schnauzer Hell (BRIAN)

've worked at some impressive homes during my career, but this one took the cake. First, I pulled up to the gate and buzzed the house from the intercom. A video camera scanned us as I chatted with someone on the other end. Slowly, the massive wrought-iron gates swung open.

The driveway curved around through perfectly manicured lawns, making the house invisible from the street. A six-foot stone wall ran off to either side—around the whole perimeter, I supposed. As my car rolled slowly down the gravel drive, crunching as it went, a mansion came into view. The driveway encircled rose gardens bursting with color. Three gardeners were tending those roses as we parked in front. Off to the left of the house, two other gardeners worked on the shrubs. Not a leaf or a twig would be allowed out of place on this lawn.

Before I could ring the kitchen bell, the door swung open and the smiling face of a uniformed woman greeted us. Behind her, I heard frantic barking and scrambling on tile, but no dogs appeared. Somewhere close by were two Giant Schnauzer puppies.

As I stepped into the kitchen, the pups came into view. I was momentarily stunned. These two pups were chained to the wall on one-foot-long chains. Both pups, a male and a female, were scrawny to the point of being painful to look at. I have seen better-looking dogs in remote African villages. Their coats were dull and dry-looking. The dogs were running in place, trying to get to me.

Mrs. McGill swept into the room. "I'm so glad you could come. We are having such trouble with these two," she said, nodding her head at the pups. As it turns out, they had employed another trainer, who had recommended chaining the pups to the wall. He felt this was much more humane than crating the pups. I am in strong disagreement with this. A crate allows the pup to get up, turn around, and make himself comfortable. And I have seen dogs get their legs caught in a chain, panic, spin, and dangerously tourniquet off the leg.

This "professional" also recommended feeding these large-breed puppies one meal a day of a light diet food to minimize defecation. In his eyes, this simplified housebreaking. Not only is this cruel and medically unsound but it created real monsters. When I used food reward for some simple puppy training, they took the food and most of my hand with it. Normally, I immediately teach a dog not to take food so roughly, but for these starving pups, that lesson would have been cruel. First, they had to get on an adequate diet.

The owners weren't trying to do the wrong thing: In fact, they were actively trying to do the right thing. But they knew nothing about raising dogs, and when a professional comes in and tells you "Do it this way," it's hard to believe that you, as a novice, know better. For the record, if your gut instinct tells you something is wrong, don't do it, no matter what expert tells you it's okay. There is almost always another method with which you will feel more comfortable.

The McGills had grown suspicious when this man had said, "Use your right hand for feeding the dog. Use your left hand for hitting the dog." They had protested his throwing heavy objects like phone books and sterilized bones at the young pups. But when, in a rage, he threw the little female more than ten feet across their yard, they fired him.

Which brought these pups and these responsible people to us. Now the McGills had two pups who were like wild things, climbing on tables, leaping up at counters, and snapping at food in desperation. They were not housebroken and the female was now growling at strange men. Not a pretty picture.

From my perspective, this was all made worse by the breed. The Giant Schnauzer is a dog with a rocket in his pocket. An energetic, athletic, intelligent, and protective combination, a Giant can be a challenge for the experienced owners and a poor choice for most novices. Two pups from the same litter are always a handful to raise; two Giant Schnauzer pups are more than I would ever recommend. For that, I blame the breeder, who clearly did not have her puppies' best interests at heart when she sold two littermates to these kind, but inexperienced, people.

In the best of worlds, this situation would have been difficult. I returned several times. Once the pups got on a regular feeding and crating schedule, they calmed down a great deal. The male, Ricky, was a doll. Mentally sensitive, physically sturdy, he came around beautifully with humane handling. The little female, Greta, was a pistol—smart, suspicious, high-drive, quick, athletic. We knew early on that she would be better off in the experienced hands of someone who had the time to focus on her fully.

This household, no matter how well intentioned, with the mother out and about every day, the father a high-powered corporate executive, and the pups overseen by a competent but somewhat disinterested housekeeper, was not the place for this breed of dog. As the training progressed and the pups grew, the McGills came to see our point. They were looking for a pair of easy dogs to blend into their household with nary a ripple. Giant Schnauzers enjoy causing ripples. After serious discussion, we all decided that these dogs would be better off someplace else.

The breeder was not interested in taking Ricky and Greta back, a sure sign of someone in dogs for the bucks, not the breed. Working with Schnauzer Rescue, we got both placed. Rescue put Greta with a family whose first Giant Schnauzer had recently died of old age. They were well equipped to handle this little fireball.

The more laid-back, sweeter Ricky went to a handicapped boy to be his constant companion in school and out. He was a huge hit in his new role.

The McGills, who had tried to do the right thing by going to a breeder, then calling in a training professional, certainly could provide a good home for the right dogs. We suggested they consider adopting two retired racing greyhounds. These elegant adult dogs would thrive on their four-acre fenced-in property and look fabulous lounging on matching dog beds. We hope, for all concerned, they took our advice.

Merry Christmas! (BRIAN)

It may sound exciting to have the largest dog-training facility in New York City, but it really is a lot of work.

Work starts at seven in the morning and goes to eleven at night, seven days a week, 365 days a year. Caring for other people's animals, as anyone who has done it knows, is stressful at best. Are the animals safe? Healthy? Anxious? Depressed? Stressed animals are more prone to disease, and disease is a kennel operator's dreaded enemy.

Sarah and I ran a good facility. Among ourselves, we called the Family Dog Training Center "Buns of Steel Dog Training." Over two thousand square feet, the center was on the second floor of a veterinary hospital on the Upper West Side. We housed up to twenty-five dogs at a time and we walked them all four to eight times a day—depending on their age and need. On a good day that meant one hundred walks, one hundred sets of stairs a day.

Here's what a normal daily routine looked like:

At 7:00 A.M., we entered the kennel area, no lights, no talking to the dogs. The goal was to keep the dogs as calm as possible. First order of business was to get the puppies and excitable dogs outside. This was always a quick walk, as the dogs didn't waste time after a good night's sleep. Pick up after each dog, jog up the stairs, take out another. Our days always kicked off with this brisk aerobic workout.

Once all the dogs were walked, general playtime ensued. Since we cared only for dogs we knew well and because city dogs are normally extraordinarily well socialized, most of our charges got a nice long communal romp on our rubber-matted, fifteen-hundred-square-foot training area as we cleaned kennels and supervised their play.

Playing was more than just fun for the dogs, it was a necessity. In our residential area, we could not afford barking. Therefore, we managed for contentment—not only because we wanted to but because we had to. We learned quickly how to make stressed dogs happy. In short, the secrets were routine, plenty of exercise, and clear rules.

After playtime came breakfast and a nap. Puppies got another walk after breakfast. By the time all dogs were cared for, the room was cleaned up, the dishes washed, the training dogs worked with, and the phone calls answered, it was time for the midday walk and romp. And so it went, until lights-out at 11:00 P.M.

The majority of the time, our staff shouldered the bulk of this hard work, but over the holidays, when we were filled to capacity, we often had the place to ourselves. So it was the Christmas of 1990.

The kennel was packed—twenty-five dogs of various breeds. Our help were with their families. We were already hustling to get everything done when the canine version of Montezuma's revenge hit at 1:00 P.M. on Christmas Eve.

From that moment, we never stopped walking dogs. We'd get through the group once and some other poor animal would be circling in her crate in the doggy equivalent of crossed legs. It was exhausting, but who had time to notice? A dog whining in the crate, telling us that if we didn't get him out in less than two minutes, one of us would soon be scrubbing out a fouled crate, was a mighty big incentive to keep moving.

I'm sure a man out there with a nice white Cadillac still has not forgiven me for accidentally allowing one of these dogs within range of his spotless car. The whole neighborhood was understandably unhappy with us. Here are some typical interactions:

I am hustling a dog across the sidewalk, trying to get him into the street in time. Miserable animal doesn't make it.

Irate neighbor: "That's disgusting. Clean that up!"

"I'd love to, but with what? A spoon?" Does this person think this is my idea of a fun holiday? Then I realize my anger. I take a deep breath. Calming slightly, I add, "I promise I will bucket it."

I run back upstairs, toss Pepto-Bismol down the dog's throat, as per the veterinarian's instructions. The dog shakes his head, getting hard-to-remove pink goo on his chest, his ears, me, the walls, the floor. I put the dog back in his crate. Wiping myself off as best I can, I then fill a bucket with a Clorox/water solution, grab another uncomfortable dog, jog downstairs—hair uncombed, jacket half-zipped, shirttails flapping, covered with smeared pink stuff. Dog gets very sick at the curb.

A woman in a fancy car with New Jersey plates views this gruesome event through a tinted window. I can see her head rocking back and forth as her stomach contracts in dry heaves. She rolls down the window. "That's the most disgusting thing I have ever seen!" she complains, the breeze having no effect on her hair-sprayed coiffure, although it does send a ripple through her fur coat.

"You don't get out much, do you?" I shoot back. The light changes and she speeds off. Ridiculously I yell after her, "This is New York City! This is nothing!" I realize I really need a nap.

BRIAN KILCOMMONS / SARAH WILSON

Picking up the bucket, I slosh both the newest puddles with the bleach solution. That serves to break the disease cycle, clean the sidewalk and calm the neighbors.

Fortunately, that year we didn't have a white Christmas. It was warm enough that we didn't have to contend with stuff freezing.

The next day, we got a wonderful Christmas present. The dogs all started to feel a lot better. The medication was helping. The veterinarian downstairs confirmed that we were through the worst of it. While not the most pleasant holiday I ever spent, it was one of the most memorable.

Emergency! (BRIAN)

As I chatted with the Smiths after a lovely lunch, I caught Sarah staring at their sweet black Newfoundland, Britain. Though the Smiths wouldn't notice, I knew something was up. I caught her eye. She gave just a hint of a shrug, then turned back to the dog.

Clearly nothing she could put her finger on. I looked at the hulk of a dog—he looked okay. Then he lowered his head a bit, ever so slightly teetering. Was he about to vomit? "I'm taking Britain outside." Sarah interrupted our chatting. "I think he's going to throw up."

"Maybe he ate something when he was out for his walk," Mary Beth suggested. George and I had just returned from a stroll among their exquisite flower gardens. Britain had joined us, sedately, as was his way.

"Maybe . . ." replied Sarah as she headed for the door.

She didn't turn to say this or excuse herself. She was focused on the dog. When she's focused like that, there is usually something the matter.

As she stood with Britain on the stone patio outside the kitchen door, I kept watch through the window as I carried on the conversation. I glanced toward the kitchen for a minute to chat as Mary Beth got a fresh cup of tea. When I turned back, Britain was gone.

"Brian!" came Sarah's frightened voice. The Smiths and I bolted for the door. Britain was stretched out on the gray stones, motionless. "Bee sting, must be a bee sting!" Sarah shouted. I ran to the dog. The Smiths stood there stunned. "Mary Beth," Sarah yelled. "Get the car. Now!" Mary Beth stood a moment longer, then ran up toward the garage.

George and I grabbed the dog, which wasn't easy. He weighed close to 170 pounds. Passed out, the dog's deadweight was immense. Sarah went ahead, opening the gates and holding the doors. He was in the car in less than two minutes. "Call ahead," I instructed Mary Beth. She reached for her mobile phone. "Tell them a bee sting is coming in."

George himself suffered from a bee-sting allergy, so he knew all too well that we had no time. Land Rovers aren't known for their speed in most parts of the world, but they are now in one small Westchester community. The vet was, thankfully, only ten minutes away. That day, he was five.

Sarah rode in back with Britain, giving us constant updates on mucous-membrane color, pupil condition, breathing, and pulse. She was calm, but her voice was sharp, demanding. Raised by a volunteer fireman, she had been trained from birth to handle emergencies. Calm or not, I could tell she was worried. I turned from consoling Mary Beth to looking at Britain. Sarah's and my eyes met again. She stared for a second, giving me the tiniest of head shakes. It was clear she did not want to cause the Smiths more distress, but it was equally clear that Britain was in real trouble.

The Rover skidded on the gravel of the animal hospital's driveway. We hustled the dog in en masse. "The doctor is in with a patient right now," the receptionist stated politely, pointing to the seats in the tidy lobby. "You can wait there."

"No," I called out to her over my shoulder as we walked past her into the exam room. A West Highland puppy was on the table, being held by his owner as the doctor peered into one ear. Both the doctor and the client looked up in surprise. "Get out," I told the Westie's owner in my best command voice. Taken aback, he scooped up his pup and hustled out the door.

We laid Britain on the table, parts of his mammoth body spilling over every edge. The doctor opened his mouth in protest, then took a good look at the dog. "Anaphylactic shock," Sarah stated. "Maybe a sting of some sort." Grabbing some instruments, the doctor agreed.

"Seen a lot of stings this week. Ground wasps . . ." His voice trailed off in concentration. The danger was immediate and life-threatening. He got right down to work.

His skills saved Britain that day, but just barely. He still tells the story, every time the huge Newfoundland comes in for routine work. "Five minutes," he says, voice softening, shaking his head, stroking the dog's tablelike back with one hand. "Another five minutes and I couldn't have helped him."

Hiding the Evidence (SARAH)

Fran adored the sixteen-month-old chocolate Labrador she had named Mimi. Mimi was a happy, fun-loving, sensitive dog who never really fully grasped the concept of housebreaking. Well, that's not completely fair. She grasped it okay, but when she became stressed, which was frequent, the concept slipped her mind. This was not aided by Fran's penchant for changing the dog's diet, or her husband's general intolerance of this behavior. Mimi did the best she could.

Fran's parents had a designer home in Connecticut, where they lived a designer life with their perfectly behaved Cavalier King Charles Spaniels. These matching little black-and-tan perfections could do no wrong. Fran got quite a bit of parental teasing about Mimi's exuberance, which turned to serious chiding when Mimi left paw prints on the windowsills, tracked mud into the house, and other perfectly normal, if unacceptable, young Labrador behaviors.

Fran knew that the housebreaking problems, if they ever occurred at her parents' home, would get Mimi banned for life. So it was with horror that Fran stumbled upon the unmistakable evidence in the center of the woolen-carpeted back hall. Her horror turned to terror as she heard her father climbing the stairs that led to the scene of the crime.

As he drew nearer, Fran breathed faster. Her palms began to sweat. There was no time to get a paper towel or even a piece of newspaper. Mimi would be banned. Fran did the only thing she could think of—she scooped up the poop, rolled it up in her shirt, put her arm across it, and ducked into the bathroom just as her father came around the corner.

"Hi, Dad," she said casually as she shut the door behind her. She heard her father stop outside the door and inhale deeply. "Ah, Franny, is everything all right?" His voice was full of concern. Fran stifled a giggle. "Oh, yeah. I guess something didn't quite agree with me. Maybe the egg salad. But I'm okay, Dad, promise."

"Mm . . ." responded her father as he headed down the hall. As far as any of us knows, her father is none the wiser to this day.

Never Board a Dog Named Litigation (BRIAN)

Murphy's Law operates when you care for other people's pets, resulting in immutable conditions that take effect with startling consistency. Any of you readers out there who are in the pet-care business will find these familiar. They are as follows:

1. No matter how long a dog's stay is, he will cut himself, develop a cough, get crate nose (rubbing the top of his nose raw from sticking it through the grate on the crate or pen), or develop a nonspecific

intestinal complaint and/or a raging hot spot within twenty-four hours of going home. The possibility of these occurring rises if:

   a. the dog has been with you a long time, in perfect health throughout.
   b. the owner is highly attached/neurotic/emotional or simply brand-new to your facility.
   c. you have just hung up the phone after chatting with the owner in glowing terms about how well the dog did during his stay.

2. The most aggressive dog in the kennel will need daily medication that he can't or won't take with food.

3. Potential clients will drop in for a quick look at the facility just after any of the following:

   a. A dog has experienced stress diarrhea.
   b. Muffy, in run three, just vomited up her breakfast and will be eating it while you are showing the people around. Possibility of this more than doubles if Muffy is a friendly bearded dog.
   c. A dog who has boarded with you many times without a hitch will catch his foot in the gate of his pen in some unimaginable way and be yelping when the clients pull up.

4. If major electrical or water-main work is being done by the town, although they will promise to come multiple times, they will actually show up, unannounced, and shut off the water and/or electricity on the morning after a four-day weekend, when

most of your kennel population is going home and most of your regular clients are picking up. The possibility of this more than triples if a twenty-four-hour stomach bug has raced through your kennel, leaving almost every dog desperately in need of a bath.

5. The dog you take in as a favor for the friend of a friend will:
   a. have a cough.
   b. have some undetermined scratching accompanied by hair loss.
   c. be a chronic barker.
   d. be dog-aggressive.

6. If a dog is to get lost, it will be the shiest one in the kennel. If the dog is to get seriously lost, it will be one of the shiest dogs you've ever boarded.

We have hard proof of this last one. In our collective forty-plus years of dog care, we have had only one animal escape us, a young Akita who trusted no one but her owners. Sumi did not want to be touched or handled in any way by us. Even after a few stays—when most dogs drag their owners into our kennel to say "Hi!"—this dog still did not consistently enjoy our petting. Occasionally, she would allow some physical contact, but it was random and always brief. She never offered any aggression toward us, but then, we respected her space.

Athleticism was not Sumi's strong point. She was a trotter and a lounger, not a runner and a leaper. Her owners concurred with this. She sometimes had to be helped into the car, as the jump up just seemed too much for her.

To lessen both her stress and ours during her stays, we left a four-foot lead on her when she was outside. This allowed us to get hold of her without unduly frightening her by actually having to touch her.

Other than her omnipresent fear, she was an easy dog to care for—mouse-quiet, a regular eater, no fence fighting with the other dogs. We were happy to have her.

Her owners were two devoted dog people. Offering their pets the best of care in every department, they rarely boarded her and worried when they did. We felt honored that they trusted us with their sensitive Akita.

After an uneventful weeklong board with us, the owners called. "We're home. How'd she do?"

"Great!" we exclaimed. "She did just great!" (See Murphy's Law, number one.)

"Wonderful. We're on our way."

"She'll be waiting." I hung up the phone with a smile. Such nice people.

I called down the kennel stairs to Glenn, our kennel manager at that time. "Glenn, let's get Sumi bathed; her people are on their way." I turned and went to the sink. Smiling to myself, I glanced out the window, checking on the dogs in their runs. All looked well. Apparently, Glenn already had Sumi in the tub. Impressive.

"Wow, you're quick," I called down to Glenn casually.

"What do you mean?" Glenn replied from the kennel office.

"You got Sumi so quickly," I answered.

"What are you talking about?"

"Glenn, where's Sumi?"

"Out in the run, on the end. Where she always is."

"No, she isn't." My heartbeat sped up. Glenn was at the bottom of the stairs instantly.

Glenn is one of the most responsible people we have ever had in our employ, and we have had some great ones. He made it from the bottom of the stairs to the outside runs at lightning speed. I shot downstairs, checking all the crates. No Sumi!

Then I ran outside to stare at the empty run and Glenn ran in to stare at the empty crates. No dog. She must have climbed the fence. It was our worst nightmare.

Glenn raced to his car, speeding off to search the neighborhood. This didn't hold much hope, as directly across the street from us was Highland State Park, all 3,500 acres of it. Worst of all, she was dragging a lead. She could get tangled in a bush. We might never find her.

I filled Sarah in and left her to make up LOST posters. I headed into the park. "SUMI!" I yelled at the top of my lungs. "SUMI, COME!" As I stood listening for the sound of leaves rustled by four running canine feet, it struck me. Sumi—sue me—yikes! Our neighbors must have thought this an odd thing to be bellowing in the woods.

We put up over three hundred posters within a matter of hours. We'd notified every dog officer and shelter in a twenty-mile radius and questioned every living soul we came across in our endless driving around the area. We offered a large reward, which in our rural community really motivates people to help. Sarah even called a friend who is a gifted astrologer. She told us that the dog would be found soon, in perfect condition. We all hoped she was right.

A friend who does search and rescue with his dog came up to give it a try. His dog made a noble effort, but she was trained to find humans, not other animals. She just never quite understood what we were asking of her.

The owners were distraught but wonderfully kind. They stayed in the area, hunting high and low. They bought a mobile phone so we could all be in constant contact. They were tireless.

We got calls from all over. She had been sighted five miles east on the far side of a major road. The next call reported her miles west, across two more heavily traveled highways. Always dragging her leash. Always, miraculously, safe. But never allowing anyone near. If anyone was to rescue her, it would have to be her owners.

Each time a call came in, they would rush out to the area of the sighting. Standing hopefully at the side of the road, they called out to their dog—sometimes happily, trying to lure her in, sometimes in frustration that yet again she was so close but never came. Maybe she was gone by the time they got there. Maybe she was too frightened and disoriented to respond. As the days crept by, we all, quietly, imagined the worst.

But fate—or God—or luck smiled on us. On the last day that Sumi's owners could stay to search, five days after she had escaped, we got a call of another sighting. They raced to the spot. Again, she was not there. On the way back, as the evening fell, her people got lost on the winding back roads of this country town.

Utterly confused, depressed, grieving for their beloved pet, more than a bit testy with each other after another disappointment, trying to get back to their hotel, they made yet one more wrong turn, and there, trotting down the center of the road, dragging that tattered blue lead behind her, was their Sumi. Opening the car door, they called her and in she hopped, as if she was just out for a stroll. Tired, a bit skinnier, but none the worse for wear, she was fine.

The next day, we took the money we had put aside for a needed used vehicle and sunk it into thousands of dollars of improved fencing. It was worth every penny.

OUR TEACHERS

Barbara Woodhouse (BRIAN)

Barbara Woodhouse rode one of her favorite cows like a horse. This cow even jumped low obstacles with Barbara on board. A lucky bovine, she was taken in a trailer on vacations to the seaside with the rest of the family. To say that Barbara was eccentric would be to understate the case. But she was also, without contest, the most gifted person I have ever seen with animals.

Her mother called the tone Barbara used to speak to the animals "her little voice." And animals, regardless of species, responded. Besides the cow she adored and the thousands of dogs she worked with, she spent ten years in the Argentine breaking horses for the British army.

We met while I was working as an associate producer for a PBS special with Roger Caras. We were at Westminster and my task of the moment was to locate dogs to have on the program. After several of the animals were used on-camera, Barbara looked up, locked her steely gray eyes on the director, and said in her crisp English accent, "Who's selecting these dogs?" I stepped forward. She nodded at me. I took that as approval.

After the shoot, she told me what nice dogs they were and asked me how I had known which to pick. We got to talking. Later that evening, at a dinner party hosted by Roger and Jill Caras, we continued the conversation. She invited me back to the Essex House for more dog discussion. I eagerly accepted.

I have no recollection of how we found a Lhasa Apso at eleven at night in the Essex House, but we did. Up and down the hotel hall we went as I watched, then tried, and she corrected and directed in her brusque manner. Barbara was a no-nonsense woman who was a gifted, caring teacher. She demanded the absolute best from her students, both human and canine. She was harder on the human because we were the ones in control of the situation. Barbara had zero tolerance for watching a person annoy a dog with incompetent handling.

Some people were put off by her direct manner, but after years of my father's verbal onslaughts, I didn't even notice her tone. Since she wasn't calling me useless, stupid, fat, slow, dumb, ugly, mean, or hopeless, I didn't even register it as abrasive. I just soaked in all the information she was offering.

Barbara didn't simply train dogs; she danced with them. They pranced next to her, eyes looking up adoringly, waiting for any opportunity to please her. She got this response in minutes, sometimes seconds. It astounded me then. It impresses me still. For me, watching her work, dog and human in respectful but joyous communion, was the essence of the best our two species have to offer each other.

At that time, Barbara was suffering from a bad back. Remember, she didn't become famous until her seventies. As energetic and youthful as she was, seventy is still seventy. The people organizing her North American tour approached me about joining them so I could assist Barbara. I said yes before they finished asking me.

Barbara was many things, none of them tactful. At the Sportsman's Show in Toronto, a huge trade show attracting thousands of people, she chided one poor woman in front of the crowd. "Love," she stated with a smile, "you walk like a chicken about to lay an egg. Why don't you try walking normally." The crowd roared. The woman blushed five shades of red. I'm sure she still cringes when she thinks of that day.

I cringe a bit myself, because for years I have wrestled with my tone. Being raised with fierce talk all the time, I thought that as long as I wasn't saying mean words, I wasn't being mean. Only now, after years of feedback and working on myself, have I come to realize how hard I must have been on some people. Though I got the correct tone with dogs almost immediately, the proper use of it with my human clients took much longer.

From Toronto, we went to Chicago. There we had a live show to do, a half-hour show, with Barbara as the only guest. The show's producer decided that five or six large dogs would be on the set at once and that Barbara would work them one after another. I recall telling him that she would not do that.

"Yes, she will," he replied confidently, puffed up by his twenty-two years of life experience.

"If I were you, I would reconsider that tone with her." The young man stared at me for a minute, then turned to go find Barbara. He did. I saw them converse. I watched her face grow incredulous. I overheard her say, "This is utter bilge" as she started gathering up her things.

Any time Barbara said, "Utter bilge!" or "I wouldn't touch that with a barge pole," someone was in deep trouble.

The producer came to me flustered. "What is she doing?" he asked.

"Looks to me like she is getting ready to leave," I replied.

"She can't! This is a live show."

"Better talk to your host about filling the next half hour." His face fell. Live TV, no guest—a nightmare.

"Can you stop her?" he asked, trying to sound casual.

"Maybe," I replied honestly.

Walking over to her as she stuffed her leads and collars fiercely into her sensible canvas case, I stood for a moment, listening to her muttering about bilge and barge poles. I waited for an opening. Taking the only tack that had any hope of working, I pointed out how her sudden disappearance would reflect most poorly on her. This got her attention, as she was a woman of honor who took pride in her reputation. She paused, made a face as though she had just sucked half a lemon, and reconsidered. It worked.

We then both went to the producer and told him what she wanted. He opened his mouth. "This is my show," he began. Barbara stiffened. I raised my hand. "This is the way it's going to go, *if* it's going to go." I looked at him intently. He got the hint, then nodded slightly.

Barbara went on, doing her usual unusual magic with dogs she had never before seen.

Barbara was a guide in my life in more than one way.

Not only was she a brilliant trainer; she was a complete inspiration. After fifty years of training dogs, after being rejected by every publisher in England and being forced to self-publish what turned out to be her best-selling book, then driving around Britain self-distributing her work to stores, she became an overnight success on the BBC.

It was at the Chicago Anti-Cruelty Society demonstration that I finally got it. I was working a Samoyed/Siberian mix who was complying, but that's about it. I could not get the dog to connect with me. Impatiently, Barbara snapped, "Give me the leash and watch." Seemingly the instant she touched the leash, the dog was transformed.

At that moment, I understood. I put it all together, that winning combination of attitude, teamwork, having fun with it, and being clear in body, mind, and voice. You don't *make* the dog do it; you make him *want* to do it. From then on, it was the difference between technique and art, marching and dancing, talking and singing, being formal and having fun! Barbara gave me an understanding of the possibilities between our two species that I could never have gotten in any other way. I will always be deeply indebted to her.

Sarah's Childhood Curse (SARAH)

Much to the mystery of my parents, I was born loving animals. My fascination with them was immediate and complete. No doll held my interest unless I could get it to ride one of my many toy horses. Where other girls played house, I played stable.

When I was an infant, our family had a Standard Poodle named Cocoa. She had a fascination with pulling off my diaper, which led to her exile from our house. With dog trainer's hindsight, I suspect she was done a great wrong.

Chances are good that Cocoa, having had several litters, was only trying to keep the family's most recent young one clean. I doubt she had any ill intentions.

Our next dog, Hannibal, died under the wheels of a car. I am told he and I were inseparable. I imagine that was true. After that, my parents refused to have any more dogs, despite my constant begging. They compensated by allowing a long parade of cats, rabbits, guinea pigs, snakes, hamsters, gerbils, finches, and, finally, a long-awaited horse.

As a child, I figured all good people in the world were fond of animals. When, one night, I caught my frustrated grandmother tossing a friendly but sleep-depriving cat out of her room, I screwed up my face and spat out the worst possible curse I could imagine. "Grandma, you are not an animal lover!" Well, actually, because of an auditory/speech disorder, it came out more like "Grwama, youw nob an ammimal luber!"

There. It was said and there was no taking it back.

My exhausted grandmother had no idea what I had just accused her of, but from my serious expression and hands-on-hips stance, she got the gist that it was nothing good. As the story goes, she tried to explain herself, but in a four-year-old's eyes, such actions cannot be explained.

My speech problems encouraged my attachment to animals. They never teased me, lectured me on not talking baby talk, or stared at me as if I were somehow less than a person. Until I got speech therapy, I frequently felt on the outskirts of the things happening around me. The feeling haunts me still, and I react now almost exactly as I did as a child: I seek out the company of animals.

As a little girl, I was constantly picking up cats who "never" allowed themselves to be handled or riding horses who "usually" threw riders. I was told I had a way with them. I think, more accurately, they had a way with me.

As I matured, I lost some of that easy connection of shared emotional response and have spent much of my adult life seeking what I took for granted as a child. I could feel them. Sometimes, today, I still can.

I have to credit my mother for her encouragement of a fascination she did not share. When I would go downstairs before some important dinner party and tell her I was training my gerbils to pull a cart of matches around the room, she would listen intently and then tell me that would be charming.

I hope, as a mother, I can emulate that ability to support the ideas without listing all the reasons why they couldn't or wouldn't work. For the record, I never did manage to train a gerbil to pull a cart, largely because I could never get the harness to fit right. But the attempts entertained me.

If we are predestined to do things in our lives, I was predestined to spend mine with animals.

Irish (BRIAN)

My grandmother, Nana, was many things, and in the instance of acquiring our dog Irish, she was a tactical genius. She told my mother that a friend of hers in Jamaica, Queens, wanted to meet all of us children. Thinking this charming, Mom bundled the four of us up on my sister's sixth birthday and off we went.

When we arrived, it wasn't long before we were all shown the litter of mixed-breed pups in this friend's basement. My mother didn't want a dog, but what possible hope did she have against four sets of hopeful blue eyes and her only daughter pleading, "Pul-llease, Mommy. Pul-llease . . . "?

My mother relented and my sister selected a pudgy little tan-and-white male pup. On the way home, we all discussed names. My mother said, "We're an Irish family. How about Irish?" It stuck.

Irish grew up to be one of the world's greatest dogs. This was the 1950s, when unneutered dogs ran loose in the neighborhoods, fathering pups and tipping over trash cans, and no one thought much about it.

As he matured into his shaggy Benji look-alike self, he would sit at the end of our driveway when school let out. All the kids knew him, waving and calling out when they walked by. His tail would thump in greeting, but he waited. When we rounded the corner, he would go into spasms of joy, leaping, licking, yodeling, making us feel safe and welcome.

My mom used to say, "The only thing this dog can't do is talk." He was never a problem. He had his routine. Wake us up, beg for breakfast under the table, see us off to school, step next door for a second meal, patrol the neighborhood, bark at the white dog down the street, whom he hated, fight him if possible, see if any of the local females were in heat, mark his territory, and hustle back home to meet us for lunch.

He was, in every way, a member of my family. During a time when my life was full of stress, terror, and unpredictable cruelty, he offered a harbor of love and sanity that I drew on daily.

My father's violence escalated through the years, focusing largely on me. Later he would tell me, in a rare moment of insight, that he came after me so often because I reminded him of himself as a youngster and he did not want me to turn out as he had.

He should be pleased that I did not, but not, I think, because he intimidated and beat me almost daily. If anyone can take credit for me heading away from violence down other paths, it is my mother, my grandmother, and my dogs.

Those years in my father's house did have value. They turned out to be a great gift to me as a trainer. I can feel aggression before a dog even knows he's thinking about it. I also have great empathy for any animal on the receiving end of brutal methods. While other people may dislike working with aggressive dogs, I enjoy it. I know exactly where they are coming from.

Irish, who lived a long life, died in my mother's arms. She heard him retching late at night. Getting up and turning on a light, she saw him quivering on the living room rug. Blood was seeping from his mouth. She knew in her heart that this was the end. She woke up my brother Michael and my father, Pete. Michael came and helped her, stroking his old companion as Irish's eyes glazed and his breathing slowed. My father stood in the doorway to the living room, saw the dog, his wife, and his son, then turned away and went back to bed.

I was not home that night. My mother called me the next day and told me the news. Decades later, I found out the real story. For reasons known only to him, my father told Sarah the truth at one of their first meetings.

Apparently, he came home from work one night loaded and angry, neither of which was unusual. When Irish came out to greet him, he kicked him. He told Sarah that the dog then crawled off under a bush. That night, Irish died.

Sixteen-Hand Teachers (SARAH)

I was one of the millions of little girls smitten with horses. At five, I was riding regularly. At eight, I was at a camp for horse-obsessed girls. Other people have detailed memories of childhood friends and school buddies; I have such memories of horses.

If you want to know who taught me about working with animals, besides Brian and my dogs, it would be Monty, Rusty, Firefly, and many other horses.

Monty was my dream horse. A huge warm blood (meaning a cross between a bulky draft animal and a lighter riding horse), a mountain of an animal, he was mostly white, with tan splotches. With his wavy mane and tail, he looked like some knight's charger from the Middle Ages.

As big as he was, he was sensitive, which is why most

people hated to ride him. If you were sloppy on Monty, he threw you—a long way down. But if you were respectful and gentle, Monty would give you the ride of your life. His trot was like coiled steel gliding across the field. Each massive hoof landed impossibly gently as he flowed forward into the next stride. There was nothing he couldn't jump, but you had to stay off his mouth, keep your legs quiet, and reseat yourself in a balanced, smooth way or he would stop, drop his head, and off you would pop like a kid down a slide.

I adored him. He, I think, adored me. Though I have not thought of him in years, I choke up a bit as I write this. A great teacher comes so rarely. He taught me that in the best of worlds, each party is both the teacher and student. That respect is the foundation of control, real control, where the animal willingly and joyfully complies with your wishes as you willingly and joyfully attend to all the feedback being sent you, whether it be through reins or leash. Harsh force may win you a momentary victory, but it may also gain you long-term resentment, distrust, and lack of cooperation— and, in Monty's case, a quick drop onto the hard ground.

After one such fall, my tiny riding teacher strode over to me, slapping her riding crop against her leather boot in annoyance. Looking down into my ashen face as I lay flat on my back in the field, she offered no sympathy. "And what did you do wrong?" she inquired without a smile.

In her world, and in the world she helped me build, it is the human who makes errors, rarely the animal. To this day, if a dog does something I do not want, I ask myself first and foremost, What did I do wrong? Usually, I don't have to look far for the answer. I didn't set the dog up for success; I hurried through too many steps at once; I misjudged speed, distance, or the dog's level of understanding. The list goes on and on. You will rarely read the words *stubborn, stupid,* or *difficult* on my list of dog problems. Those catchall phrases usually mean poorly trained, incorrect methods, rushed, frightened, or misunderstood.

A Springer Spaniel comes to mind. I was watching a local competition obedience class. A woman with an English Springer Spaniel was working on sit/stay after several minutes of intense and, in my book, overly harsh heel work. She told the sitting dog to stay, then stepped out into the end of her six-foot lead, where she was going to turn and face her dog. As she stepped out, she inadvertently gave a tug on the lead. She did not notice this, but her dog did. After the previous lesson of being yanked about for heel work, he was sensitive to all lead pressure. Thinking that she had just made it very clear that he was supposed to get close to her whenever the lead got at all tight, he stood up, taking a step or two in her direction.

When she turned and saw him standing, her face became a mask of rage. Striding the few feet back to her hapless companion, she yanked the lead up, giving the dog a harsh correction. "No," she snarled. "Sit!/stay!" The dog sat, ears lowered, eyes lowered, hunched in his spot. She lost a lot at that one moment: his faith in her leadership, any sense of safety he might have had. He had no place to go, no way to stop this confusing and painful process. His one option would be to become aggressive, which I've seen happen more than once, and when it does people say, "Out of the blue! For no good reason! We were just training like we always do and he snapped."

Clearly such people did not have my riding instructor. She taught me about these matters early and well. She taught me, and so did a chestnut pony named Rusty. Here's an animal I do not miss a bit, but I still respect him for all he enlightened me about, mostly as I argued with him.

Rusty was a classic school pony, which means he had been ridden for so long by people who knew so little that he had taken matters into his own hands. This was fine under most circumstances, because if ridden clearly with no options offered, he responded just fine. However, the camp I attended was not a big believer in stirrups, and often we rode without holding the reins, as well, and though that taught me to stick to a saddle like glue, it gave Rusty way too many possibilities.

If Rusty had been a dog, he would have been a terrier. As Rusty taught me, it is useless to argue with those who enjoy a good fight. Force was ineffective with him, unless you used a tremendous amount (this was the 1960s, when violence was considered the norm at many stables), at which point he would obey physically, while he waited for the merest hint of an opportunity to turn the tables on you. His bag of tricks was extensive: He might nip your butt the next time you went to mount up, stop dead from a canter, attempt to scrape you off on a fence post, or take you low under a branch. Patience was one of his virtues and revenge one of his arts.

Harassing an animal into compliance—be it a dog or a

horse—is no great accomplishment. It brings with it little grace or beauty and nearly always costs you the animal's participation in the process. And it's the animal's participation that takes any performance from routine to spectacular.

The wonder of good training is teaching the animal to want to comply, so that he brings everything he can to the action he is doing. The best dressage horses float across the ring with a contained power that can make you gasp. The best obedience dogs perform the same way, floating beside their handlers at heel, racing in when called, leaping in the air with joy at the release. Such animals are in true partnership with their people. That partnership is my training addiction. Once you have had it, with any species, even for a moment, you can never settle for less ever again.

Tara, aka T. (BRIAN)

A dog of my own had been on my fifteen-year-old mind for a while. My mom had promised me, "You save up enough for half of what a puppy will cost, I'll chip in the rest." Inspired, I grabbed a job at a furniture-refinishing place for the summer and saved my pennies.

When I had enough, I went to the local pet store—yes, pet store, I didn't know any better. A big-eared Vizsla puppy caught my eye, but she was a bit timid. That was the breed for me! After arriving home, I called every local pet store looking for my new dog. A place out in Huntington, Long Island, had a male.

The man working at the store tried to talk me out of

him. "Vizslas are stupid. They can't be trained. What you want is a German Shepherd." "No," I retorted, "what I want is that puppy." Even at fifteen, I was not easily swayed.

I named him Tara. The dictionary said it was Gaelic for *earth*, which seemed right, given his rich red-brown color. Later, when my brother Mike pointed out that Tara was a girl's name, I shortened it to T.

T. was a thinker. If he wanted something, he sat quietly next to me, staring into my face. It was impossible to ignore his unwavering jade green eyes. I'd ask him, "Do you want water? Do you want dinner? Do you want a walk?" When I got to the right question, he would nudge me or bark softly.

My mom and he had an adorable routine. He would bark at her. She would say, "Don't you give me any lip." Of course, he would bark. Then she would complain, "You always have to have the last word," and he'd woof. He made us all laugh, which is a great gift in any life.

One evening, when T. was a little over a year old, my father started in on me. I forget what it was about, but it doesn't matter anyway—he always had a reason: I was too smart or too stupid, or I did well on a test or I did badly, whatever. The fight was at the verbal stage, but it was heading rapidly toward the inevitable physical violence. I was attempting to retreat up to my room, but my father would have none of that, cornering me at the staircase.

He was a construction worker. He tied steel all day. His hands were like bricks; his arms, bundles of steel-hardened muscle. He could still send me flying. As he became more irate, T. began to growl. Lying against the kitchen door, ears flat back, T. rumbled. My sister went to put him in the den. She didn't want him to get hurt, but T. wouldn't go.

He pulled away from her, slowly stalking across the room like a cat, coming to a stop between my father and me. He half-crouched, motionless, eyes locked on my father, every hair on his back erect. He vibrated with fear, rage, and determination. This both further enraged and somewhat surprised my father, who stared at the dog for a few moments, then looked at me.

I was no longer a boy and I knew in my heart that if he hurt T., I would come after him. All at once, my father knew it, too. Turning away, mumbling something about "that damn dog," my father went to the kitchen, sat down, and cracked open another beer. I slumped back on the stairs, weak-kneed. Putting his front paws on my lap, T. licked my face while wagging small, happy wags. I buried my head against his neck, smelling his warmth and dogginess. We had won. Together, we had won. As long as T. was with me, my father never came at me again.

That was not the only time my Vizsla stepped forward in my defense. When driving out to study prevet at Iowa State one year, I took T. along for company. I was a long-haired hippie type then. When I stopped at a truck stop along one of the endless midwestern highways, a cowboy-booted, beer-bellied, John Deere–capped local boy took an instant dislike to me. I believe he said I was an "East Coast longhaired asshole faggot."

Because he was such a big man, I felt he had a right to his opinion. However, he did not feel I had the right to leave quietly. He followed me to my car, making numerous rather creative comments about my family, my friends, my beliefs. I continued to ignore him. T. did not. I opened the car door and T. took his stand between me and the stranger.

"What the hell is that, you—" asked the man.

"That's my dog," I replied.

"What does this candy-ass little dog think he's going to do to me?"

"He thinks he's going to bite you, if you keep hassling us."

"I'll kick him from here back to that hippie East Coast you come from."

"I wouldn't do that," I suggested coolly. He snarled soundlessly at me, then drew his tugboat-sized cowboy boot back, taking aim at T.'s ribs with his pointy toe.

Snake-quick, T. pivoted sideways, then came at him. Jaws snapping, he rushed our harasser, harrying him at crotch level. The man instinctively jumped back. Once he was out of what T. considered to be my space, the dog stopped, holding his position but offering no other aggression.

The man may have been ignorant, but he clearly wasn't stupid. He made a few more nasty statements before retreating with a swagger that did not nearly match my dog's as T. trotted off to lift his leg on a nearby oak.

Firefly (SARAH)

My father made good on his promise of a horse on my fourteenth birthday. Money was tight then. My folks had just divorced, so it was with no small sacrifice that he honored his word. I didn't realize then all that must have been involved financially and emotionally to pull it off, but I can make some pretty good guesses now. Thanks, Dad.

As, I am sure, my friends will heartily concur, I am fascinated by control. I used to get my control jollies by working with hard-to-manage animals. I got over that in my twenties, but as a youngster, nothing thrilled me more than riding an almost-out-of-control horse. So when Firefly threw me on my first ride on him, I was sold. My father was not so convinced, but I talked him into it.

As the old Chinese curse goes, "May you get what you wish for," and I did. The general consensus around the barn was that Firefly was gelded late, which means he was castrated after he understood what his landing gear was for.

He tried to climb out of his stall to get to mares in season. In retrospect, I wonder if he had a retained testicle, because many of his problems seem to be testosterone-based. At the time, I thought he simply needed love and lots of training.

He was barely 14.2 hands, which, in the horse world, made him a pony. The year I got him, I shot up to my adult size of five feet eleven inches, making us a ridiculous couple. If I stretched hard, I could touch my toes together under his belly.

Firefly planted seeds of understanding in me that would not ripen for well over a decade. He showed me the importance of creativity in training, and the necessity for accepting an animal for who he is and not for who you want him to be. These two concepts are pivotal in all the training I do today.

BRIAN KILCOMMONS / SARAH WILSON

A retired school horse, Firefly had developed tricks to avoid being ridden. One was to spin when I tried to mount him. For weeks, I attempted to make him stand still. This proved impossible. No fourteen-year-old girl is going to make a horse do something he has no intention of doing. Attempting to force him to stand created all kinds of frustration in me, which led to yelling, bit yanking, and neck slapping, none of which increased his understanding of what I wanted. It did increase his tension about being mounted, which caused him anxiety and, in turn, led to more spinning. My emotional, violent response had increased the behavior I was trying to stop. Word of advice: If the problem you are trying to correct is getting worse, rather than better, stop what you are doing! Try something else, learn another method, talk to someone more experienced, or hire a professional, but for heaven's sake, stop!

One day I just gave up. I held the reins just behind his jaw and said, "Fine—spin. In fact, I want you to spin." Whenever he slowed down, I urged him faster. After a minute or so, he came up with a fabulous idea. Could he possibly stop? He'd very much like to try standing still. So he stopped and I mounted a stationary horse for the first time.

Eureka! That day, I got it! I learned that some of the most effective training happens when you set it up so the animal can't help but do what you want; then you allow them to do it. Follow the animal's decision with immediate, sincere reward, and you are on the road to success. In Firefly's case, I allowed him to stop, which was, indeed, exactly what he wanted most.

It worked brilliantly. After that, I rarely had a problem getting on board, and if I did, I simply made him spin a couple of times, which always refreshed his memory. He then stood like a statue. Lesson number two, which Brian would reiterate years later: Good training gets immediate results.

With this newly acquired knowledge, I tackled his next-most-annoying problem. Once I was on his back, he often refused to walk. Instead, he threw himself into reverse. The more I urged him forward with my leg, the more he backed up. Next time he did this, I said to him, "Fine, buddy, let's go backward," and around the ring we went, tail-first, as fast as I could make him go. After several minutes of this, I allowed him to stop. Then, with the loosest rein and a gentlest nudge, I requested forward movement. Off he walked. A miracle!

I have applied this same principle to dogs many times with equal success. Barking for attention is my favorite example. A dog barks for my attention; I say to him, "Fine, you want my attention? You now have all of it! Sit, down, sit, down, come, stay, okay, sit." Then I proceed to make him work rapidly. I demand quick response and offer little, if any, praise. After a minute or two, I drop the leash, resuming what I had been doing. Normally, the dog decides that my attention isn't exactly what he wants, preferring to go off to chew a bone or nap in the sun.

Firefly was a difficult animal, but, like many of the most difficult animals I have worked with, he taught me an incredible amount about effective training, himself, and, key to all this, myself.

Beau (BRIAN)

T., my beloved Vizsla, had died years back. It takes me a long time to get over losing a dog. But now I was ready for the next "best dog I've ever had."

Another trainer I knew had a Rottweiler, a nice dog, but not an easy one. The dog impressed me with his intelligence, his raw strength and attachment to his owner. A good Rottweiler is an amazing animal. Properly bred and raised, they are the kind of equal companion that is hard to find in the canine world, but they are not easy dogs to own. Beau did not change my opinion about this. He was—and the breed is—high-maintenance. With Rottweilers, training is a lifelong project. You, as the owner, do not relax or let them have their way. You uphold the rules. In a positive but inflexible way, you insist on compliance. You work on their responsiveness constantly. Even with all this, they will still, occasionally, check who's in charge.

Beau checked—about every six months. One day, for no apparent reason, when I gave a down command, he would simply look at me, fully understanding the word, yet testing whether I meant to enforce it. When I did, he would lower his eyes as if to say, Okay, okay. I'm a Rottweiler; I have to keep checking.

"Down" is an excellent behavioral thermometer. If a dog who thoroughly understands the command and complies consistently suddenly stands there staring at you, something is up, and whatever it is, it isn't good.

But I'm getting ahead of myself.

I set out to find myself a pup. I spoke to many people involved with the breed and one name kept coming up—Mrs. Muriel Freeman. Muriel is the grande dame of the Rottweiler. Devoting her life to a breed she initially thought of as ugly, she is now a world-renowned dog-show judge. She has even graced the center stage at the most prestigious dog show in the United States—Westminster.

I came to know her first and best as a Rottweiler breeder. My first inquiry about a pup was answered with a curt and unyielding *no*. She did not sell to dog trainers because they would attack-train one of her dogs, something she did not approve of. A good Rottweiler will lay down his life for his owner, but that type of training she considered both unnecessary and bad public relations.

Determined, I pressed on. I would not do that kind of work with her dog. I had excellent references. She listened. She checked my references. She called me in for a meeting.

Sitting in her library in her well-appointed apartment on the East Side of Manhattan, I met the woman herself. Lean, perfectly coiffed, with intense eyes, she got right to the point. Who was I? What was my experience? What was my training philosophy? Answering to the best of my ability, I was beginning to wane after three hours of intense questioning. Throughout it all, her beloved Rottweiler Graff was at her side. Every interaction Graff and I had, she watched closely. In the end, she allowed that I might meet her pups but she still made no promise that I might actually have one. They were up in Westchester. We set up a visit for the next Saturday.

That Saturday, I arrived at her kennel complex. Graff and Muriel came out to meet me. As she ushered me in, she said, "Your puppy's in this litter. Pick him out." With that, she swung open the door to the puppy yard, allowed me through, closed the door behind us, then stood on the steps, arms crossed, waiting to see if I knew what she knew about these pups.

They were all husky, outgoing, gorgeous examples of their breed. I was in a male-dog pattern then, having had Irish and T. before. Now I have three adored females in our family pack, but then I wanted a male. One by one, I picked up the males, cradling them, stroking them, reading their reactions. The third one I picked up was a large male in this already-large litter. As I cradled him, he lay absolutely relaxed in my arms, not the least bit concerned about his position. When I looked down into that adorable puppy face, he met my gaze head-on. Through my hand resting on his inverted chest, I could feel the growl coming. Then I heard it. Relaxed, confident, and a pain in the ass, this one had to be mine. I turned to Muriel. "This one," I stated. She nodded curtly and smiled. I had chosen correctly.

For those of you out there looking for puppies, this is *not* what I recommend you select. For a novice or pet household, such a response is very, very bad. But I was not a novice or a pet household; I wanted a strong-minded dog and knew I would have no trouble with his level of assertion.

With constant training and careful socialization, Beau grew into a magnificent dog. He and I shared a bond that included his anticipating my desires. Commands were often issued wordlessly and immediately complied with. Confidence exuded from his every pore, meaning he did not start altercations but was more than willing to put an end to them.

One night, when I was walking him late in Central Park by the West Sixty-ninth Street entrance, he was off sniffing some doggy thing ahead of me. A couple of gentlemen in dark ski caps and hooded sweatshirts stepped out of the bushes and asked for all my money. Soundlessly, Beau trotted to me, stood between me and the strangers, and started to expand. With every intake of breath, he grew in size, till he stood on his toes, every hair on his back up, his eyes staring, his intent unmistakable. With every exhalation, a wet snarl vibrated through the night. The men left. Beau watched them go. Slowly deflating, he shook himself thoroughly, looked up at me for the okay, which I gave him, and off he trotted for more olfactory investigation.

In the wrong hands, he would have been a menace. But we formed a team that worked well for six years, till his death—a team that I think I will never match again. When he succumbed to cancer, a chunk of my heart died with him. We were part of each other's souls. I don't know how else to explain it.

Picking Up Urs (SARAH)

As we flew over to Germany on our honeymoon, Brian made a casual comment about maybe seeing a dog we liked on this trip. This launched me into a one-woman tirade about how people travel to Germany for years without seeing anything they like and/or that is in their price range. Germans have quite the reputation for attempting to unload their less-than-desirable dogs on the unwitting foreigner. Anyway, we had our two females, whom we adored, we didn't need another, and adding an unneutered male was out of the question. We occasionally bred a litter, and having such a dog around when our girls came into season would be stressful for everyone, especially us. It was a real Bible-thumping diatribe, which Brian sat through with good grace.

Needless to say, I was the one struck with Cupid's arrow at the second kennel we visited. We were just there visiting friends of our interpreter. These friends were longtime Shepherd breeders who kept seven or eight Shepherds in a converted greenhouse next to their home. As the man walked us through his kennel, a sixteen-month-old male caught my eye. Not really my eye, more my heart. Friendly behind the chain link, he licked any fingers offered. The soft look in his eye and the eager wagging tail impressed me.

As the others in our party oohed and aahed over two adorable young pups, I wandered back to this gawky adolescent. After several more minutes of watching him, I went and tugged on Brian's sleeve. "Ah, sweetheart," I said, "check out this male." Brian looked surprised but had the good sense not to say anything. He liked the dog, as well. The price was right. The deal was done, and I will eat crow for the rest of our life together.

In fact, originally, I skipped this part when I wrote this

story, but Brian insisted I share it with you. It's penance I deserve, and anyway, who cares. The dog is wonderful. But back to the story.

Once we returned home, sent the checks, arranged for transport, the big day came to go retrieve the dog, whom we dubbed Urs, from the airport. The U.S. Customs area looked like some kind of betting operation. Rows of windows stretched down both sides of the room. Behind these windows, people worked, heads down. There were no lines. Only a few men were there getting help. I stood in front of one man to ask for some guidance, as signs were not to be found. He was chatting with another worker. He looked up, made brief eye contact with me, then continued his conversation. After a minute or so, I butted in. "Excuse me. I'm importing a dog from Germany. Where do I need to go?" The man pointed to his right but never stopped conversing.

Lovely.

With relief, I spotted a female face. Moving to her, I got everything I thought I would need ready and in hand—papers, money, wallet. Speaking through the tiny hole in the thick Plexiglas barrier between us, I began, "I hope you are the right window. I'm importing a dog from Germany today and need the paperwork. . . ." The neatly dressed person looked up, and while she didn't exactly smile, she at least was helpful. "Put that money away," she said quietly as she bent to the task of sorting out the papers. "Oh." I tucked it into my hand, out of sight. Right, I thought, glancing around the office. New York, seedy office—stupid to advertise anything.

"Do you have ID?" she asked me curtly.

"Yes." I handed her my passport. She did what she had to, then handed it back. Bored and anxious to get this all done, I started tapping the passport on the desk. Glancing up quickly, the worker stared at me for a second. "Put that away," she said slowly, as if I might be mentally limited, then glanced around the room. I shoved it back in my pocket. I, too, looked around. No one seemed to be paying any attention to us, but I took her word for it, one woman to another. From then on, I kept everything out of sight.

Finally, papers completed, stamped, and otherwise official, she sent me on my way. Now I was in a "hyperalert female in a male world" mind-set. The hall from the office door to the elevator was dimly lit. I didn't like the blind corner by the elevator. I didn't like how, when the elevator opened, I'd be out of sight of anyone in the office. I took a deep breath. Nothing is going to happen, I told myself. You're just spooked. I gathered my wits about me, rode the elevator uneventfully, and made my way to the cargo office.

The cargo office at John F. Kennedy International Airport in New York has the ethnic diversity of a United Nations meeting and the sexual diversity of your local lumberyard. Men with baseball caps, yarmulkes, and turbans all slouched in plastic chairs, waiting for their cargo to arrive.

Finally, after over an hour's wait, I was told to go out to the loading dock. Urs's crate was rolled out on a dolly. Looking inside the darkened interior, I saw front legs braced against sudden movement and a large red-and-black head pressed up against the roof of the carrier. Stepping forward, I spoke to him kindly. No response.

About then, I began to contemplate the fact that I now had a big dog I did not know in a crate on an open loading dock at JFK International Airport. I tend to dismal thinking anyway, and the parade of possibilities for the next five minutes of my life went as followed:

- Urs bolts, getting hopelessly lost in the airport.
- Urs bolts, heading straight onto the highway only a couple of hundred feet away.
- Urs panics when a stranger reaches for him, and bites.
- Urs panics and refuses to exit the crate.
- Urs panics and defecates all over himself before a two-hour ride home in a small car.

I took a deep breath. Turning to the men gathered inexplicably close behind me, I made a small suggestion. "Ah, you may want to step back a bit. I don't know this dog well." They scattered.

Turning my attention back to the dog, I chatted happily. "Urs, buddy. How about we go home?" He did not move a hair. Uh-oh. Peering into the crate, I laughed. "Come on, buddy. How you doing?" Not a tail twitch, not an ear movement. My throat tightened. In an ordinary situation, I would leave such a clearly stressed dog alone, but that was not an option. My little car would not hold a crate this size, and even if it could, I had no way of getting it to my car loaded as it was with an adult German Shepherd. I'm a strong woman, but I'm not that strong. Urs had to come out.

Bracing one knee behind the door so I could block any

attempt to bolt, I eased the door open enough to reach in. Thankfully, the breeder had left a collar on him.

Urs remained frozen as I reached in. I laughed, trying to relax him. Touching him was like touching a furry cinder block. Every muscle was tight. All the blood left my hand, my wrist felt constricted, and my fingers felt fat and awkward. I fumbled with the lead. The clip kept slipping out of position. Many times in work with animals, the mental must override the raw physical instinct. My body was telling me, Retreat! Run! My brain won the coin toss, though.

I sang nonsense to him as happily as I could. No need to let him know I was nervous. Finally, the lead in place, I stepped away from the crate, allowed the door to swing slowly open, and waited. This was no time for yanking; he was stressed enough. Nothing moved inside the crate.

Bracing myself against the possibility that he might launch himself forward, I gave a gentle tug while praising him enthusiastically. Something stirred. I waited a few more seconds. Cautiously, he stepped out, splaying slightly as he hit the slick cement floor. He looked around, ears forward, tail in a relaxed position. Disoriented but fine, this dog clearly did not have aggression on his mind. I stroked him calmly on the back, but he paid no attention. He scanned the room, apparently looking for a familiar face. I was just one more unknown person in an unknown land after an inconceivable trip. Why should he say hi? Who was I to him?

I peered over the edge of the loading dock, four feet down. I scanned left and right for stairs. Nothing. "Miss," called a dock employee. "Use the stairs inside. It's the only way." Thanking him, I led Urs back into the office.

I pushed the grubby door aside and entered the stuffy room once more. All heads turned. Urs—head down, tail out stiff—was still trying to negotiate this uniquely slick surface. Leaning against the lead, scrambling for balance, he looked, to the unknowing, like a dog struggling to get free—about seventy pounds of gorgeous, muscular German Shepherd struggling to get free.

If it is possible for a whole roomful of strangers to act in unison, this room did. Everyone, even people on the far side of the room, drew back a few inches. Men sitting with their arms draped over the backs of the empty chairs on either side of them, legs wide apart, brought their arms to their laps, their knees together, and sat up straight. No one, except perhaps a Catholic nun, could have caused such a metamorphosis. I grinned for the first time all day. Nothing like a good dog, I said to myself as we headed out of that dim, grim building into the bright fall sun.

Urs and I walked in the weeds edging the parking area for a few minutes, giving him a chance to relieve himself. Still nervous, he peed while walking, leaving a loopy trail of copious wetness behind him.

At the car, I offered him some water, which he gratefully accepted, but still he wouldn't make real contact with me. How scary it must be to fly to who knows where, landing in some strange country and walking off with some person you only dimly recall. I looked at him sympathetically. "In time, Urs. In time. I promise you, this will all make sense."

Opening the CRX's door, I flipped up the seat and told

him to hop in. No hop. He froze again. Clearly, he saw this as one more vehicle in a long line of vehicles. "Okay," I said to no one, "point well taken." I lifted his stiff front legs in. Thankfully, once he saw the inevitableness of the moment, he clambered onto the back deck. I clipped him into the cable I have mounted in back, and we headed off.

He lay down. I chatted pretty much nonstop at first, figuring he could get to know my voice. I offered him a biscuit, which he politely took but didn't eat. No whining, no panting, no struggling—this was a dog of character. When I glanced back at him, he was checking out the traffic, not looking at me. So I shut up and let him be for half an hour or so.

After the first tollbooth, I offered him another biscuit, which he took and this time ate. A few minutes later, I reached back and offered him my hand. *Thump, thump,* his tail whomped on the floor of the car. He licked my hand softly. I glanced back and his eyes met mine. "Hey, buddy," I said. "Welcome. . . . Welcome home." I turned back to the road; he put his head on his paws and watched me.

ONLY IN NEW YORK

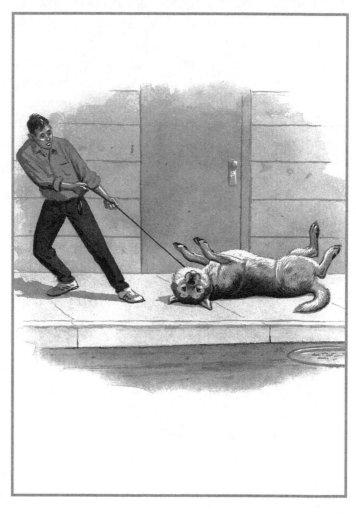

The Dumbest Dog We Ever Trained (BRIAN)

People frequently tell us their dogs are dumb. We usually correct them, explaining that the dog is actually confused, untrained, mistrained, or otherwise undirected. The majority of the dogs we see are extremely smart. They have conquered the challenge of controlling a human household, have developed ways of getting their needs met, and have made the humans who serve them think it was all their idea to begin with. That's smart.

Redwood and his owner, Bart, were another matter altogether. Redwood was a pet-store Malamute. We don't claim to know his whole parentage, but he had a mighty small head for the breed and his eyes crossed disconcertingly when he concentrated. Malamutes are normally an intelligent breed. Redwood was the exception that proves the rule.

The presenting problem was that Redwood, at a hundred-plus pounds, would not walk on a lead. His idea of coping with the situation was to lie on his back and be dragged. Dragging a one-hundred-pound Malamute with all four feet skyward down East Seventy-eighth Street was becoming an embarrassment for Bart. Redwood seemed to enjoy these little jaunts. He would play bow with his chest on the ground and his butt in the air, give a huge mischievous grin, then flip himself belly-up.

Bart had tried everything he could think of by the time we arrived, from long drags (Redwood enjoyed this), to bribery (Redwood had little interest), to encouragement (Redwood would get up wagging but flip himself over the minute forward movement began).

We solved it in a few minutes by introducing Redwood to curbs. While sliding a couple of inches from the sidewalk to the street posed no real physical dangers, it did startle him. He had not taken this possibility into account.

We walked at a steady pace, chatting enthusiastically about life and letting Newton's law of gravity work out the problem for us. Redwood got up. We stopped and had a praise party with him. He wagged all over. He was an inordinately sweet dog. It was over. He got the message. We all walked back into Bart's apartment building. The doorman gave us a thumbs-up sign, nodding his approval. I smiled back.

We then went into Bart's apartment to discuss some chewing problems they were having. The apartment was furniture-poor and box-rich. Corrugated cardboard boxes were everywhere. For those of you who do not know, corrugated cardboard is, apparently, great fun to rip up if you are a dog. Almost as much fun as toilet paper, paper towels, or newspaper. Redwood enjoyed it, as the scraps of cardboard everywhere attested.

Glancing around the room, I spotted a puddle of dried urine on the floor. Now, a Malamute pool of urine is a major thing, maybe the size of two large pizzas. It spread in the area of Bart's bedroom, bathroom, and kitchen entrances. It must have been hard to miss when fresh.

"Bart, there is a puddle of dried urine in your hall."

"There is?"

"Bart, it's huge. How could you have missed it? This has to be cleaned up."

"It does? Why? It's dry now."

"Because Redwood will smell it and go there again. Anyway, Bart, it's gross."

"The maid comes on Thursday." (This was Tuesday evening.)

"It needs to be done now. Do you have a mop?"

"I've never used a mop."

"It isn't complicated." So not only did I get to introduce one dog that day to walking but I also had the honor of teaching one obviously sheltered young man the art of mopping.

As Redwood's training progressed, it became increasingly apparent that he was a special-needs dog. He tried hard. He wanted to please. He just couldn't remember things. He also had a hard time pinpointing sounds. If you called him, he tended to spin, cocking his head from side to side as he tried to figure out where you were, even if you were a mere ten feet away. In fact, when he came to stay with us for a few weeks, he got lost in our small, fenced backyard. He could not remember where the back door was located. When called, the poor thing would pivot in place, unable to process the information. We simply got in the habit of walking out to get him.

Working with him went like this:

"Redwood. Sit."

Eyes crossed, he pauses. Wait, he seems to say. Wait, I know that word. Sit . . . sit . . . Hmmm . . . Oh, yes! That's right! Sit! And he does, tail wagging, with a big grin of accomplishment. I did it. Right? This is sit. Right?

"Good boy, Redwood." I pat his dense skull, shaking my head slightly. "Good boy." I try to speed him up a bit, but it becomes clear that pressuring him in any way is simply cruel. His delay is not due to any type of resistance; he just is not very bright.

About this time, Bart laid out his grandiose plans for his dog. Redwood was to go to the elevator, press the button, wait for it to arrive, enter the elevator, press the button for the lobby, get out at the lobby, and get Bart's mail.

When I stopped laughing, I broke it to him that, for Redwood, learning his name was a long-term goal. Basic commands like sit, down, come, heel, and leave it would need constant review to maintain at any functional level, and if Redwood ever did get to the lobby on his own, he wouldn't remember what he went for or where he'd come from. He was a delightfully happy dog, without a mean bone in his body. That was a gift in and of itself and would have to be enough.

Dane Drain (SARAH)

Boarding Chester is both a pleasure and a burden. Owned by two of our favorite people in the world, he is always tended with a level of care bordering on the neurotic. Great Danes are known for their delicate constitutions, especially under stress.

At the time of this story, Chester was a mere ten months old, ninety-five-plus pounds, and a sensitive sweetheart. Keeping weight on a growing giant breed is often a challenge, Chester being no exception. He was lean, as he should be, but if he dropped weight, he would careen right into scrawny. I couldn't stand the idea of seeing his owners' expressions if he returned to them looking like a prisoner of war. I wanted him to eat.

Chester had different plans. He was fasting. This was not a big problem; we know many tricks to get a dog to eat. The simplest one is to add a bit of wet food into their regular dry meal. Just a tablespoon of canned food mushed in with his six cups of dry tempted him enough to eat. This pleased me, but now I had another problem.

Danes are prone to something called bloat. This horribly painful condition caused by the stomach filling with gas and closing off is not common in young dogs, but we wanted to be careful. Stress and a change in diet are two triggers for this condition. It's the kind of problem that kills dogs in just a few hours. Leaving him at our training center was not acceptable. I knew I wouldn't sleep well if I couldn't see him, so Chester came home to our apartment.

Our home sweet home was a twelve-by-sixteen-foot studio two blocks north of the center. This sounds small, I know, but it was a step up from living in Brian's even smaller office at the center itself, where we had lived for almost a year. After all, this twelve-hundred-dollar-a-month hole-in-the-wall had heat, a shower, and a kitchen, which was more than his office offered.

At this point in our lives, we normally worked sixteen-hour workdays, seven days a week—at the kennel at 7:00 A.M., home after the last walks at 11:00 P.M. This Saturday was special. We could sleep as late as we wanted in the morning because Linda, one of our talented trainers, was sleeping over. She would handle the morning walks. We could laze in bed till 8:00 A.M., maybe even 8:30. This was the first such break in months. Those of you who have pushed yourself this way with infants, business, or school know that there is nothing like a break in sight to bring all the exhaustion you've been forcing to the back of your mind into full awareness. We walked Chester home with us, stripped off our clothes, and crawled into bed. Sleep claimed us both almost before our heads hit the pillows.

Minutes later, Chester's whining brought me back to consciousness. He stood, expectant, at the end of our bed. Clearly, though inconceivably, he was an on-the-bed dog at home. Not here. I had a whole nine hours ahead of me, and I didn't want to share it with a gigantic, restless puppy.

"No, Chester, go lie down," I told him firmly before flopping back down to luxuriate in a sleep-induced coma. I knew he had gotten the message, because the last thing I remember hearing was Chester turning around and around, in preparation for lying down. I was asleep before his elbows hit the king-sized dog bed.

More whining. Bleary, I was near tears as I looked at the clock—1:42 A.M. My night, my one precious night, was slipping away. Trying not to wake Brian, I whispered harshly at the wide-awake Dane: "No! Chester, go lie *down*!" He dipped his sensitive Dane head, pulled his ears sideways, and slunk off to his spot. Brian didn't stir. I don't remember lying back down.

At 3:27 A.M., I lost my patience with our demanding charge. Leaping from bed, I grabbed him by the collar. "Chester." I glared at him eye-to-eye just inches from his huge Dane nose. "This is my only night to sleep. I am exhausted. This is not home. You are not getting on our bed. Now—*go—lie—down*." I shook the collar briskly; he shot back to the dog bed, eyebrows arched in upset. Feeling that now, surely, I had made my point, I stalked back to bed, cursing his indulgent lifestyle.

At 4:43 A.M., I awoke to the sound of water running. As I battled back to consciousness, I realized it wasn't water running, but a hose being turned on. We didn't have a hose in our apartment. Did a pipe break? What could possibly—I pondered, then opened my eyes. Tripoded two feet in front of my nose was the business end of a Great Dane with diarrhea.

For several moments, I lay there staring. I knew better than to move. This pile was epic enough. I didn't need to surprise him, making him walk off midway through, leaving a trail behind him. I was such an idiot.

Chester had tried to warn me. When he finished, he glanced back at me, then skulked under the table. "Oh, Chessie," I apologized, going over to him. My heart contracted. What a fool I was, what a self-centered fool. "This isn't your fault. You tried to tell me." I stroked his smooth bony head. He didn't look at me. "I'm a jerk," I mumbled to myself. "A complete jerk." I turned back to the matter at hand.

Our tiny studio apartment smelled like someone had gutted a moose in it. I am an old hand at cleaning up disgusting dog by-products, but this was off the scale. I glanced back at Brian. He slept on. I thought about waking him, but why? How would that help? I decided to be a kind partner and let him sleep. I figured he'd wake up as the cleanup got going.

The mass had the size and consistency of a spilled bowl of cake batter. Carefully, I edged by it, going into the kitchen to get a roll of paper towels. Reaching for them in the dark, I felt hard cardboard tubing. One sheet was left. I squatted down and quietly opened the cabinet below the sink. Touching the contents quickly, I felt no more paper towels. I groped around for rubber gloves. Then I remembered I had taken them over to the training center.

Sitting back on my haunches, I cursed softly. "Damn it!" At least we had the *Times*. Newspaper wasn't perfect, but it would have to suffice. Carefully opening the paper, I peeled off several sheets. Using the paper, I scooped up as much as I could. Carrying the load in front of me like a ticking bomb, I headed toward the garbage can.

It was pitch-black in that windowless end of our tiny abode. I could just make out the edge of the can by the door. As I bent to deposit my armload, I sunk up to my ankle in another warm pile. This one, sprawled across an old Oriental rug, dwarfed the one by the bed. I gagged.

Brian slept on.

Hobbling toward the bathroom on my heel, the ball of my foot raised high, my body convulsing, I looked like a one-woman conga line. I will not repeat what I said, but it had a wonderful four-beat cadence and involved a parent. Sorry, Mom.

Because of the airflow patterns in this stuffy apartment, or the lack of them, the bathroom was a stink-free oasis. With one foot hovering under the faucet, my back braced against the wall, I scrubbed between my toes. Long after the last traces disappeared down the drain, I scrubbed. Finally, the pain of skin abrasion made me stop.

Opening the tiny window next to the sink, I sucked in fresh air like a drowning woman. Refreshed, I stepped back into the main room.

I addressed the mess by the bed first. Several sections of the *Times* later, after much paper rustling and plastic bag wrestling, the floor looked like the scene of a bizarre finger-painting accident. Brian slept on.

Grabbing the corners of the Oriental, I dragged it past the bed. I glared at Brian's motionless form. How could he possibly sleep through all this? Was he faking it? Brian's soft, even snores convinced me otherwise.

Grunting a bit, I maneuvered the folded rug through the narrow bathroom door, then wrestled it into our ancient lion-footed tub, turning on the shower. Foul brown water ran out from the bottom edge of the carpet. I sat, hunched over, defeated for a moment. The hell with it. The rug could go. It was never going to be the same anyway. I turned off the water and left the rug propped against the side of the tub to drain.

Standing in the safe zone just inside the bathroom doorway, I looked at Chester. He lay curled up on his dog bed, head down, whites of his eyes showing under furrowed brow as he looked up at me. "Come on," I said to him softly. "Let's get you outside." Putting on his collar and lead, we took the elevator down to the morning. Outside, Chester sniffed the trash can on the corner; I took deep breaths. For once, the city smelled positively fresh.

Chester's mood was excellent. Clearly, his tummy upset had passed. He trotted next to me, sniffing about, occasionally looking up at me with a wide-mouth Dane smile. Not one to tempt fate, I walked him the two blocks to our office to spend the rest of his morning relaxing on linoleum, where we had cases of towels, industrial cleaners, serious mops, and my rubber gloves.

After taking a quick temperature on Chester (normal) and pouring some Pepto-Bismol down his throat for good measure, I put him back to bed in Brian's office. He had more room to stretch out in there. Satisfied that he was okay, I made my way back home to finish the grim job. By now, the sun was coming up.

When I got out of the elevator, the stench met me in the hallway. Resting my hand on the knob, I composed myself for more than a minute before entering. The first thing I heard was Brian's quiet snoring. I shook my head in disbelief. The next half an hour was spent double-bagging disgusting newspapers, then rolling up the Oriental and hauling it out the door to the trash area. Then I hosed and scrubbed the tub.

Finally, I finished the job with a mop-down. The moment the *click-clack* of the metal parts of the mop hit Brian's ear, he sat bolt upright. He took a deep breath, his lips curling in disgust as he scanned the room and then me. I stood, mop in hand, unwashed except for one foot, dressed in what I had been able to grab in the dark, glaring at him. "Ah . . ." he suggested gently, "want to go out for breakfast?"

For You—A Special Price (BRIAN)

Debbie and Ed were in their fifties. A few months back, they had acquired a Golden Retriever they named Marigold. Marigold was now making their comfortable life uncomfortable with her exuberant jumping, pulling, mouthing, running off with dirty laundry, and all the other things a normal, healthy, untrained Golden Retriever pup does.

I arrived at 1:00 P.M. It didn't take me long to get Marigold into some semblance of control, but the same can't be said about Debbie. Debbie not only asked all the questions; she also answered them. For those who have met me in person, you know that I am a hard person to steamroll, but, for the full hour, I barely got a word in edgewise. Maybe I said three or four sentences, all of which Debbie disagreed with.

Ed spent most of the hour methodically packing his pipe. He occasionally made brief eye contact with me, giving me a "What can I do?" look before he focused back on that much-fussed-over pipe. The occasional remark he did attempt to add was instantly interrupted by his wife.

By 2:15, Debbie was winding up her monologue. "So," she declared, knitting her fingers together while resting her hands on the kitchen table in front of her. "What is all this going to cost?" She looked right at me.

"Normally," I replied, meeting her gaze, "I sell a package of eight sessions for six hundred dollars—but for you, it is a thousand."

"A thousand! That's outrageous!" she protested. "Why is it a thousand?" Even Ed looked up, curious but still silent.

My eyes never wavering, I replied, "For the last hour, you have interrupted me, disagreed with everything I told you, and questioned my expertise at every turn. If I have to fight you to teach you, it costs more. I call it 'combat pay.' "

She looked aghast. Ed put his pipe down, a smile slowly speading across his face for the first time. He reached into his well-worn tweed jacket and pulled out his checkbook. "Ed!" Debbie exclaimed. "This is the most outrageous—" Ed looked at her briefly. "Mr. Kilcommons," Ed said graciously, turning back to me, "may I show you out?"

He walked me to the door, chuckling. "Here, son," he said warmly, one hand on my shoulder, while handing me the check for payment in full. "No one has ever spoken to her that way in her life. You are worth every penny." As he closed the door behind me, I saw him shaking his head, laughing to himself, muttering, " 'Combat pay . . .' "

Say a Prayer (SARAH)

I rarely fall in love with a client's dog. I enjoy them. I have fun with them. But I don't get attached. I can't afford to; my heart couldn't take it. Nor was I a big fan of small dogs before I worked in Manhattan. I thought them less of a dog somehow. I simply state now that I was wrong— very wrong.

Melinda—a tiny imp of a Maltese—utterly stole my heart. She was owned by a lovely woman on the Upper West Side who had a large, perfectly furnished apartment, a delightful and, I think, eagerly awaited toddler, and full-time help.

When Melinda came in for a couple of weeks of training, I was smitten. She was charming—as most of this breed is—smart, full of herself, humorous, and athletic. Also a cuddler, she would nestle down into the warmth of my arms with a sigh, giving herself over completely to a sound sleep. We liked each other instantly. She came to trust me completely.

When I handed the little dog back to Mrs. Reilly, my eyes filled up, my voice cracked, and I offered that if, at any time, she could not keep this dog, I would take Melinda in a heartbeat.

Once home, Melinda began exhibiting some odd behavior patterns. Eager to please at our facility on Seventy-fifth, she exhibited freezing behaviors at home. I was told that she would stand in the kitchen, shaking, refusing to move. Although problem-free in the crate at the center, she now gave her owner a hard time about crating and developed some housebreaking problems, as well.

None of this made any sense. I suggested I go over to do a follow-up. Sometimes I just can't get a clear picture of what is going on until I see it for myself. In this case, I saw a plastic Vari-Kennel with the side caved in. This is not an easy thing to do, as these are crates designed for the rigors of air travel. I asked Mrs. Reilly about it. "Oh, Maria bumped it with the vacuum." Maria was one of the two housekeepers. Bumped it? You bump a Vari-Kennel, it slides. If it was against a wall, the side might dimple but then, because of the design, pop right back out. To cave in one side—something I'd never seen before—you'd have to hit it with tremendous force. But the owner did not understand this, and Maria stood by smiling and shrugging. I had a sinking feeling.

I left some written instructions. Back at the office, I voiced my concerns to the staff. My head trainer pulled me aside. "I didn't want to say anything. I thought maybe this guy was making it up," he began. "But their driver says those housekeepers hate that dog and slap it around when Mrs. Reilly isn't there."

I grimaced. Not good. Not good at all. The whole situation was made worse when I next visited their home. This time, Mrs. Reilly's delightful little girl had a nasty purple bruise on her forehead. "She fell in the hall," Maria said. "She was being naughty, running. She knows she shouldn't run." Again that smile.

It all ended badly. When I tried to tell Mrs. Reilly my suspicions about the situation—that Vari-Kennels don't buckle easily, that Melinda's problems were the result of stress and fear, that I had heard some unsettling things about her help, that I was concerned—she distrusted my motive. She thought I was trying to get the dog for myself, trying to make trouble in her peaceful household. She dismissed me.

I asked around, but there was not much I could do. I had no hard proof. I hope that I was wrong, horribly wrong. But, late on those sleepless nights, I know that I wasn't. Say a prayer for little dogs and children everywhere.

ID Please (BRIAN)

New York is a city of experts, or, at least, of people who think they are. Here are a few of our favorite "expert" comments.

I was standing waiting for the light to change at the corner of Seventy-eighth and Broadway. Piper, our champion Scottish Deerhound, slouched against my leg as I stroked his small folded ear.

A gentleman leaned out of the phone booth he was using. "I know what that is," he proudly exclaimed, pausing for effect. "That's a llama." He was so proud. How could I disappoint him? What a great story this would make. I gave him the thumbs-up sign, returning his huge smile. "Not many people would know that," I replied. "I'm kinda an animal expert," he added modestly. He waved to us as we crossed the street.

Deacon is a male Rottweiler. While not the most muscular of his kind, he is, nonetheless, an impressive dog. People would stop us often to ask me questions about him. On an evening stroll up near the Museum of Natural History, a group of twenty-somethings walked past in boisterous conversation. "That, my friend," puffed one proudly, glancing at me with a knowing look, "is a Portuguese Water Dog." I could not help a snort of laughter. "Well, aren't you rude," the dog expert said.

"I'm sorry, but if you know enough to know what a Porty is, how could you possibly mistake it for a Rottweiler?" The group strode off insulted, with the expert waxing on about the similarities of the breeds. As if there were any. They are both dogs. It pretty much ends there. Rottweilers are black and tan, short-haired, tailless, stocky, massive dogs, usually weighing at least a hundred pounds, often much more. Portuguese Water Dogs are never black and tan, have curly hair like a Poodle, have longish tails that curve over their backs, and weigh around fifty pounds. It would be something like confusing an army tank with a Honda Civic.

One of my favorite New York conversations was with a gentleman from the East Side. He saw Piper, and commented, "Nice Wolfhound." This is a common and easy mistake, as these two breeds do look alike. "Actually, it looks quite a bit like a Wolfhound," I responded, "but this happens to be a Scottish Deerhound."

"No it's not."

"Excuse me?"

"No, I have the only Deerhound in Manhattan," he stated firmly.

"Well, sir, this Deerhound happens to be a champion."

"No he isn't," he continued. "I have the only Deerhound in Manhattan."

Piper and I walked off, leaving this gentleman clinging to his slender vine of uniqueness.

Indecent Exposure (SARAH)

The morning I moved from Manhattan to Brooklyn was a beautiful, warm March day—you know, the first day that feels like spring is more than peeking around the corner, the day you might notice a few early bulbs sprouting a hopeful green through the sea of brown. I awoke early—restless about the details of moving and excited about settling into a larger apartment. I decided to take the dogs for an early run. It was 5:30 A.M., give or take. Riverside Drive was empty, and so was the park.

It was the quiet of early morning in the city. I was

strolling along, going over my mental checklist and watching my young Bouvier, Kesl, try to keep up with our field-bred English Springer Spaniel, Sasha. Sasha raced back and forth neurotically, as was her way. If I had known more about her when we named her, I might have suggested Ion, Zip, or Cheetah.

A jogger came up the stairs from down below. Wearing a sweater and a pair of skintight tan runner's pants, he loped in front of us at a lazy pace. I admire runners, since I'm not one, and I watched him as I mulled over my coming day. The dogs paid him no mind, as they were city dogs, well used to the comings and goings of countless strangers. He kept looking back over his shoulder at me—not at my dogs, but at me. An internal city alarm went off. It was just a glance or two, but it wasn't right. Suddenly, my quiet morning walk in restful privacy seemed like an isolated, dangerous walk in an ideal ambush spot. Riverside Park is lower than the street above. Only a few staircases off to my right allowed entry or retreat up to the more populated street. The stairs on my left led to even more desolate areas. I checked around me; not a soul was to be seen. Screams would go unnoticed. I called Kesl to me.

I suppose, in retrospect, I could have turned for home, maybe even should have, but I know I have a more fully developed sense of danger than most. If I went home every time I thought I might be in trouble in New York City, I'd never go a block. Anyway, I resented being frightened, so I continued on, my Bouvier pup close beside me.

The runner slowed a bit. I responded by speeding up.

Stupid, no doubt, but I hate being frightened and that's my way of dealing. Force the hand, call the bluff, prove me wrong or right, but prove me.

When we got about fifty feet from him, he spun around, facing me head-on. I stopped dead in surprise. Turns out they weren't tight tan running pants at all. In fact, he wore a Nordic-type navy-and-white patterned sweater, sneakers— and nothing else. He stood there proudly, waiting for my reaction.

I did what any red-blooded American woman would do who was raised by two wild older brothers. I did what came naturally, and I did it without a second thought: I laughed. I laughed loudly and long, and that laugh was the only long thing in the vicinity.

I have never understood how the sight of a naked man is supposed to frighten a woman. It has always struck me as both absurd and pathetic.

My would-be impresser was crestfallen, sprinting back from whence he came in a rush. His quick movement caught Kesl's attention. I unclipped his leash, allowing him a bit of puppyish chase before the man disappeared down the steps. I knew Kesl was being playful, but I doubt very much that Mr. No Pants did. At least I hope he didn't.

Devil's Choice (BRIAN)

Is this the dog-training place?" asked the earnest, deep male voice.

"Yes, it is."

"You train dogs?"

"Yes, we do."

"Can I ask you a question?"

"Absolutely."

"Is it better to hit a dog with a broomstick or a pipe?" Pause . . . Was this some kind of sick joke? I had to assume otherwise. If it was a joke, it would play itself out. If it wasn't, this might be my one chance to save some poor creature from torment.

"Can I ask you why you hit the dog?"

"To teach him" came back the startled voice. Clearly, the answer was obvious to him. From there, we had a surprisingly positive conversation. He wanted to train the dog. The dog wouldn't listen and he knew of no other, better way to handle the situation than violence.

We talked a long time. He could not afford training and would not accept free work, but I hope that at least I planted the seeds of change. I gave him some simple exercises to do, sent him to the library to take out our book, and told him to call anytime if he didn't know what to do.

I could easily have become self-righteous, lecturing him on how wrong he was, but that would only have made me feel superior. That's no good to his dog, who is the one who needs the help in this situation.

Most people only knock on a door once. As professionals, we have one shot at making a difference. While it is more comforting to speak with people who believe what we believe, it is more beneficial to the animals we serve to discuss other options with people who think differently. I hope I made a difference.

Beware the Owner! (SARAH)

A crazy man roamed Central Park for a while. Well, frankly, there are *always* crazy men in New York City parks, but this particular crazy man was a clean-cut younger gentleman dressed in a business suit, and he fed dogs doughnuts laced with poison. Just before the incident I am about to recount, I had had a vivid, sad discussion with a woman who had lost her dog to this troubled man's handouts.

I offer you this background just so you don't think I am completely nuts.

This day, I was eating lunch at a nice little bistro in Park Slope, Brooklyn. As it was a clear, beautiful day in early fall, the large windows that stretched from floor to ceiling were open like so many doors. My ex, Peter, and I were enjoying a typical New York lunch—lots of greens I'd never heard of in the salad, sun-dried tomatoes, goat cheese, Perrier—it was the mid 1980s.

Kesl was tied to a parking meter, in clear view of the table. Midway through the meal, I glanced over to check on him and saw a strange man feeding him something. Now, I knew this wasn't Central Park, and the guy didn't have a suit on, but none of that mattered.

I do not remember leaving the table, leaping through

the open window, or crossing the ten or so feet to Kesl's side. I do remember grabbing this stranger by the shoulder as he bent over, spinning him away from my dog, prying a very surprised Bouvier's jaws open, reaching down his throat, yanking out the hunk of whatever it was, and tossing it into the street before spinning back on the man. Shaking with adrenaline, eyes blazing, I walked into his space, forcing him back, step by step. When I was about three inches away from his face, I spoke with a voice I didn't know I had. "Don't you *ever* feed my dog anything. Just what the hell do you think you were doing?" I spat the words at him, my voice vibrating with threat. His face drained of all color.

"But . . . but . . . I just saved him a little of my hamburger," he stammered, motioning with his shoulder toward the ritzy restaurant we dined in. "I'm from Illinois. I just got here yesterday. I thought he'd like it." The words spilled out of him in a tide of good intention. "He . . . he . . . he was being such a good dog."

If it is possible to go from a tiger to a worm in a matter of seconds, I did. "Oh," I said, stepping back. "Oh no. I am so sorry." I reached out my hand to touch him on the arm. He drew away. As it became clear that I was no longer the Amazon warrior/goddess of wrath, he felt safe to leave. Turning on his heel, he returned to his friends, who by now had closed their mouths.

"Everything I have heard about New Yorkers is true," I could hear him saying. "That woman is *insane!*"

I turned back to Kesl, who still looked mighty puzzled.

"You are a good dog," I told him. "Too good. I never want anything to happen to you." I stroked his shaggy head, regretting that I had deprived him of a chunk of an eight-dollar hamburger.

After my knees stopped shaking, I walked over to the man's table. Squatting down in an effort to be smaller, less threatening, I apologized profusely. I told of the recent poisonings, explaining that New Yorkers can be crazy but mostly weren't—despite my behavior—and offering to buy him a drink or maybe a few.

He accepted my apology and offer graciously, though I suspect it was more out of fear of what I might do if he refused me than because of the good, solid, ingrained midwestern manners he no doubt possessed. Then Peter and I paid our bill, collected our dog, and left, much to the relief of the management, I'm sure.

Raining Rabbits (SARAH)

In New York City, you inevitably have to deal with many things, but what you don't expect to have to deal with is four-footed wildlife. In fact, in an eighth-floor apartment, the only wild thing you ever expect to see is the occasional pigeon or maybe an uninvited cockroach.

So when Amanda kicked back on her couch on a warm May Sunday morning, coffee at the ready, Sunday *Times* spread out around her, her Scottish Terrier, Fizz, busying himself with a squeaky toy, she was relaxed. All was well with her world. Snapping the paper open to get out the wrinkles, she settled in to read the "Arts and Leisure" section.

Terrier people become immune to canine disturbance after a while. If you paid strict attention to every scurry of furry feet and every excited yip, you would never get a single thing accomplished. Fizz was into something, but it wasn't until his barking became incessant and Amanda became worried about the neighbors that she looked up to see what the commotion was about.

Out on the terrace, Fizz was barking at the small pile of wood that she kept for an occasional blaze in her tiny fireplace. This, in and of itself, was still no big surprise. Fizz had a tendency to roll his ball under there, then bark in distress until she relented, retrieving it for him. He also had trained her to retrieve his toys from under the couch.

Amanda sighed, put her coffee mug on the coffee table, laid the newspaper open on the couch, got up, and, tightening her robe around her waist, went on out.

"Fizz, why do you do this?" she said, chiding the dog. He did not look up, just dug frantically at the pile. Amanda knelt down, reaching her hand into the dark opening between the logs that Fizz was focused on. Out shot a furry projectile. Amanda fell backward with a scream. Fizz, thrilled beyond his wildest imaginings, scrambled on the concrete in hot pursuit. His barking went up in pitch and volume.

Rat! was Amanda's first thought, but since it was white and large and because she noted some pretty long ears flattened against its head as it streaked past her, she decided it must be a rabbit. Not that a rabbit appearing out of nowhere on an eighth-floor terrace made any sense, but there it was.

Righting herself, she hurried in. Fizz had jammed himself partway under the couch, which muffled his barking somewhat. Straining with his hind legs, he struggled to get completely under the couch and to his quarry. Amanda quickly grabbed Fizz's hind end and lifted her squirming, protesting terrier into the air. She carried a struggling Fizz to her bedroom, where she unceremoniously stuck him into his crate. There he vented his frustration at one of life's great opportunities lost.

Closing the bedroom door behind her, she contemplated this phenomenon. Since rabbits neither climb nor fly, this rabbit, by logic, had to have fallen. Stepping out onto her terrace, she looked up. No signs of life on the terrace above, but that had to be where it had come from.

Getting down on her hands and knees, Amanda peeked under her couch. There in the back corner, ears flattened against its smooth white skull, crouched a mighty unhappy rabbit who was no doubt wondering what he had done in his life to deserve being sent straight to rabbit hell. Carefully, Amanda pulled out the couch, slowly reached down, and took the poor thing by the nape of the neck. Lifting it up, she cradled it against her robe. After struggling briefly, it lay trembling in her arms. She stroked it, thanking her lucky stars that Fizz was not an experienced hunter. With that thought in mind, she stepped into her slippers and took the little beast upstairs.

An amazed mother and a relieved little boy were reunited with their lost pet. Though they had been hunting for it all over, they had never imagined it had sky-dived to the terrace below. Instead, they had thought perhaps it snuck out into the hall, so they had been searching the trash area and laundry room for almost an hour. The rabbit was none the worse for wear, although the whole event probably took years off his little rabbit life.

The Morning Paper (BRIAN)

'm having trouble paper-training my puppy," said the distressed female voice on the other end of the line.

This is a common city problem, so I leaned back in the chair, prepared for a friendly, if oft-told, fifteen minutes. "What seems to be the problem?" I asked absentmindedly.

"She just isn't getting it. Every morning, I get up and show her what to do, but she just isn't catching on."

"Show her?" I swung my legs off the desk, sitting up. "You mean that you go—"

"Yes, every morning. She still doesn't get it. Is she dumb?" the voice asked earnestly.

"Whoa . . ." I began, now completely engaged. My mind was racing. Did she do this in her bathrobe, hiking it up? Or maybe she dressed first? I was torn—laugh or be professional? Professional won.

"Dogs don't normally learn by watching," I said in a studied, calm tone. "If they did, they would dial out for pizza and run up our credit cards ordering squeaky toys."

From that point on we made some real headway in both

paper-training and limiting this poor woman's morning mess. Bless the devoted, if confused, owner. Her heart was in the right place, just not the rest of her.

Sarah and I figure she has to live alone. We just could not imagine the conversations if she were married. "Ah . . . sweetheart, what are you doing?"

CAN'T COMPLAIN

Midnight in Central Park (SARAH)

At our kennel, client dogs often did not get their last walk till 11:00 P.M. All too frequently, our own wonderful companions would have spent a boring day lying around the center while we attended to everyone else's ani-

mals. After a day like that, they needed space to stretch, sniff, romp, and just do dog things. Home was no place to do this, as our studio apartment was barely big enough to hold our bed and all our dogs stretched out. What they needed—what we all needed—was a serious run. For serious runs, there was only one place: the Great Lawn in Central Park.

Even at midnight, with few lights, I felt well protected. In hindsight, I think I was naïve, but at the time I felt safe with our four dogs—Deacon, a Rottweiler (ninety-five pounds); Kesl, a Bouvier des Flandres (ninety-five pounds, but his hair made him look fifteen pounds heavier); Piper, a Scottish Deerhound (thirty-two inches at the shoulder, ninety-five pounds) and Caras, an Australian Shepherd (a quick-moving fifty pounds). Totaled, it added up to 335 pounds of dog.

Running this group during the day was out of the question. Piper needed a large space to accommodate his enormous stride. Moreover, he did not enjoy other dogs clambering all over him, so he was not a candidate for one of the dog runs that provide a great service to the city.

Letting them exercise off lead en masse during the day was not an option. Not only was it illegal—a fact that deters few city dog owners—but with this group, people got understandably scared when they saw them. For all these reasons, and more, I took the risk and went to the Great Lawn after dark.

Regardless of why I did it, the dogs thought it was a grand idea. All four leaned into their leads as we turned into the entrance at West Eighty-first and Central Park West. The occasional person selling illegal substances at that corner always politely stepped aside for us to go by.

Once we turned that corner, Piper bounced his happy, slightly geeky Deerhound bounce, eager to be off. Caras danced beside me, looking up. A run! Right, Mom? A run! That's what we're doing now. . . . Kesl's nose went down, instantly disappearing into the exclusively canine world of scent, and Deacon scouted the horizon for things to chase.

On the walk down the path toward the road that circles the park, I let Kesl and Caras off their leads. These two were responsible dogs, listening well and not prone to impulsiveness. Kesl would lumber off in the slow Bouvier pace. Caras would run in forays out from us, circling back to check in, then heading off again.

Both waited on command at the road, which we all crossed together. The occasional night bicyclist or jogger would speed by. Once across, as we approached the lawn, the mood changed. Kesl would bounce in front of Piper, moving backward, daring him to run. Deacon nudged Piper from the side; Caras barked excitedly while Piper reared, ready to be off.

I got well out into the field and waited for my eyes to adjust, scouting around myself: no one. When I unclipped Deacon, he shot out a few yards, then pivoted, semicrouched, waiting for Piper to run. Reaching down the soft leather lead, I unhooked Piper. Before I could say a word, he disappeared into the grayness, the other three in hot pursuit.

On my favorite nights, a light mist lay over the grass. In the midnight silence, the sound of their breathing reached me long before I could see them: 335 pounds of huffing dog, coming at me like the hounds of hell. The sound built as they neared. Soon, I could make out their footfalls on the damp grass, like not-so-miniature horses. Finally, at the last moment, four dark shadows separated from the grayness, becoming dogs for a moment as they careened at me. I stood still as my private sea of dogs washed past me, pulled by the tide of exuberance, back out into the ocean of black.

As I waited for them to return, the clouds might give way to a nearly full moon. When this happened the light made long shadows extend from the trees ringing the field. Then I could watch my canine ballet.

Piper was always out in front, head lowered, ears back, loping at about three-quarter speed. He liked being chased. The rest struggled to keep up, their breathing labored. Piper was soundless. Their tongues lolled, flopping with every stride; his was nowhere to be seen. It was the high school track team against an Olympic athlete: lots of effort but no competition.

By the second or third loop, Piper turned on the afterburners, streaking off, leaving the rest looking as if they were walking. Kesl inevitably quit first, though Deacon was right behind him. Stopping, they watched the powerful gray rear pull away from them. Caras was good for one more lap.

If the night was cool, the herding dogs would plot a bit; doing complicated geometry, they figured where Piper would end up next, then cut him off, or tried to.

Piper liked this game. As the two black hulks, Kesl and Deacon, stampeded at him, Piper would feign surprise, dancing out of reach like an experienced matador. Both the Bouvier and Rottweiler, suffering from breed-related momentum problems, would overshoot their nimble target.

By the time they had slowed enough to turn, Piper was half-way across the field.

Caras matched Piper turn for turn, but he was such a kind soul that he did nothing when he finally caught up. Both Deacon and Kesl would have shouldered him hard, but not Caras. He barked a couple of times, then peeled off toward the center of the field to set up another chase-down.

Within twenty minutes, all four were panting like locomotives. I could have gone home, but I didn't. I stayed out a bit longer for my own pleasure, for my private reason. Empty space is to be coveted in a city such as New York. After a day of being accessible, friendly, assertive, and a resource for many people, the luxury of silence and solitude cannot be overstated. On nights when the grass was dry, this country girl would lie down, lean back on my elbows, and look up at the stars. The park is a fine place to star-gaze when you have four large dogs lounging around you like circled wagons.

With a sigh, I eventually got up, which signaled my companions to rise, as well. Kesl would shake himself. Piper would trot off to sniff some exciting smell. Caras would stretch, then look up at me. Deacon might scratch an ear. Smiling in the dark, I would call them to me, then hook them all up. Together, we would leave the field, go back down the path, across the road, and out. Beyond the entrance to the park, the lights blazed, the taxis whizzed by, and the bus brakes squealed, the city invaded every sense again. But I did not mind. I had had my privacy. I was content.

Et Tu, Cuma? (BRIAN)

Elsa Peretti, the jewelry designer, remains to this day one of my favorite clients. I wasn't at all sure how we would feel about each other at the end of the job when she explained to me that she had seven unneutered Akitas living on her mountaintop villa in Italy and that they were, no surprise to me, fighting.

Akitas are, as is written in their AKC standard, aggressive with other dogs. Keeping two of the same sex can be complicated. Keeping three unneutered males (two of which were litter brothers and the other was their father) and four unspayed females of varying ages under the same roof in peace, rather than in pieces, was a very tall order.

Add to this that Italians, in general, have extremely strong feelings about neutering anything. Even the veterinarians are vehemently opposed to it. A month in a villa in Italy sounded wonderful, but this job sounded impossible. Nonetheless, I agreed to give it a shot.

Landing in Rome, I was met by Ms. Peretti's gardener. He spoke no English and I little Italian. He stood at the door of customs, holding up a sign reading KICOLMO. I hoped that he meant me. I wasn't dead sure that I was in the right place until I stepped out of the car three hours later and was met by a couple of Ms. Peretti's magnificent dogs.

Before arriving at her villa, we came first to the gate-house. The whole establishment was built by the Romans in the sixteenth century. As we drove through the iron gates and up a mile-long driveway to the main house, over-looking the Mediterranean, I felt like pinching myself. What other line of work would have me being driven to such a place?

I started out my professional career tying steel in a nuclear power plant, like my father, and somehow I ended up being chauffeured around in Italy. Not bad. I grinned to myself. Not bad at all. Leaning back in the seat, I sighed as I watched the startling blue of the Mediterranean shift in the sparkling sunlight.

The car rolled to a stop in the circular cobblestone drive below the main house. Stairs cut out of the rock itself climbed to the villa above. I heard barking coming from behind the house, where four Akitas came out to greet me. Must have the males locked up, I thought to myself as I greeted the bitches. Friendly, nice dogs, all imported from Japan.

It was late in the day by this time. The caretaker, Antonio, laid out a wonderful spread of fresh fish, braised vegetables, fresh-baked bread, and homemade wine. We feasted as we tried to make some sense of each other. Hand gestures and bizarre facial expressions became the main mode of communication. "*Aggressione, rrr*" Antonio would say, baring his teeth at me and snapping. I nodded wisely.

"Males?" I asked, bulking out my shoulders, making myself bigger. Nodding all around. Antonio held his hand out straight, first at waist level, then twice lower down. He repeated the lower signal, then said, "*Aggressione*" and bared his teeth once more. Apparently, the two sons were ganging up on the father. And so my "interview" went.

Several cups of strong Italian coffee later, I had a pretty good idea what was going on. For years, Cuma, the oldest male, had been roaming the Roman countryside, mating with willing females and fighting all comers. He was tough, experienced, and tolerated zero lip from his sons. Now his sons were maturing. Though one appeared somewhat short legged, he was otherwise normal. When any of the four in-house bitches came into heat, which was frequent, major battles broke out among the males.

The staff kept the sexes apart and did the best they could to keep the males separate, but it was getting to be a feud. Any time the sons would spot the father, they went berserk. Daily scheduling began to look like a complicated game of bloody musical chairs. On a typical day, the bitches relaxed out on the south terrace and Cuma resided in the kitchen. The other males were down at the caretaker's house, where they would proceed to howl most of the day. Cuma, hearing the howling, hiked his leg on the door of the refrigerator in a silent response to the ruckus.

Italian or not, these dogs had to be neutered. I would await Ms. Peretti's arrival to discuss this. In the meantime, some basic control was called for. I have to say, they were all terrific dogs. I have found some Akitas a challenge to train, but these were not. They picked up on their commands quickly, seeming to enjoy the work. It took several hours in the morning and afternoon to get them all worked. After that, they slept and I was on my own.

Daily, I hiked down to the sea to swim off the diving platform or read on the sunbaked rocks. The clarity of the water allowed me to see all the way to the bottom. The rocks, large, passive solar collectors, warmed the water in the inlets, making swimming more of a bath than a breath stealer.

Sometimes I just sat in the sun, toasting, watching the yachts of the very rich proceed by in a dignified procession. After an hour or so, I would make the long trek back up the hillside for another meal of wonderfully fresh vegetables, and more, ever more, homemade wine. This was followed, as dusk always follows the afternoon, by a deep, restful nap. By the time I surfaced from that sleep, rested, content, feeling that all was right with the world, it was time to work the dogs again.

One old method for straightening out intrapack aggression is to muzzle the dogs, then let them fight it out. The hope is that once one dog wins definitively, the pack structure will be set, relieving any further need of conflict. As I watched the well-muscled Cuma trot across the upper terrace, I dismissed this as a possibility. He was an experienced fighter, he was an Akita, he was king of all he surveyed, and he would never submit. His sons, were, well, his sons. I doubted they would ever back off, either. Scratch that option.

I drew the cooling evening air deep into my lungs. Neutering would help, especially if I could get the two younger males done. That should take some of the pressure off of them and off of Cuma. Also, getting all the females spayed would eliminate the hormonal torment of almost constantly cycling females. That was the plan.

Picking up my well-used leather lead, I walked across to Cuma. "Until then, old man," I said, clipping on the lead, then scratching his impressive skull. "Until then, you have to learn to inhibit yourself." We went to work some more on "Leave it."

On lead, they progressed nicely. Within a few sessions, I could work Cuma close to his sons (who were tied safely to the iron fence) without his losing focus on me. I could work his sons while the old man was tied nearby. But I knew this was only the barest of starts. These dogs had to live together in some kind of harmony, which was an entirely different level of behavioral change.

Fortunately for all concerned, the females had not started fighting among themselves. Females who fight are often much more difficult to handle than males. Neither is exactly a cakewalk, but males typically fight to make a point. When females fight, they are usually trying to kill one another.

I stayed a month in this piece of heaven on the hill. During that time, the two younger males were neutered, as well as three of the four females. (The fourth, Ms. Peretti wanted to keep for breeding purposes.) All could be together under close supervision and in noncompeting situations. By this, I mean no food to fight over, no toys to covet, no females in season to desire. Basically, in human terms, they could sit down and watch a G-rated movie together, but that was about it. I counseled the staff never to leave them alone, unsupervised. The dogs' obedience was immediate, which gave the staff a way to direct the animals to nonthreatening behaviors when tension developed.

All in all, it was a great success in my book, much more than I had dared hope to accomplish. After all, I'm a dog trainer, not a magician.

Canterbury Farm (SARAH)

Our farm looks up at the Shawangunk Mountain Range. In the interests of literal truth, these would be called hills in Colorado. But they give us a good view. The "Gunks," as they are known around here, are covered with bare rock face that climbers come from all over the world to climb.

My personal view is that death will find me soon enough without me volunteering for it. By the number of ambulances that whiz by our house in the summer, heading up to the mountains, I can attest that this is no idle fear. Brian doesn't share my outlook. I chalk that up to a classic estrogen/ testosterone difference—the kind of difference that has been going on for thousands, probably millions of years.

"I'm going out with Joe and the guys to hunt me a mastodon," says the caveman.

"Why do you have to hunt that big thing? We have plenty of berries and roots to eat. Mastodons are dangerous," replies the cavewoman. They stare at each other as if both have clearly lost their minds.

Don't get me wrong. Personally, I am a fan of testosterone; otherwise, I wouldn't be married to B.K. I just don't always understand it.

Our farm is a bit over 150 acres—more than we were looking for but not more than we could turn away. The deal was good, so here we are, in our little bit of heaven.

We share the property with two elderly horses: Puff, a retired racehorse who has lived here for twenty years, and Misty, a mare we got from Horse Rescue to keep Puff company. Puff was part of the deal with this place. We got it largely because we were willing to look after her. She's twenty-four now and ticking along. I think we'll have her for quite a bit longer. Misty is like a Jeep. She's almost twenty and shows no signs of age other than a bit of arthritis when it gets cold.

We have some thirty ewes and two rams. Sheep are very cool, affectionate in a food-oriented kind of way. One of life's pleasures is watching them go about their sheep business of grazing, napping, chewing their cuds. The one unpleasant thing is their breath. Having spent the day regurgitating mouthfuls of fermenting grasses, if they belch near you, it can set you back.

Add to this group twelve chickens who should start laying eggs any moment, five dogs, and three cats; that's the domestic list. We are also the landlords to innumerable deer, groundhogs, foxes, coyotes, rabbits, voles, and a diverse population of birds. We manage our land for the birds mostly, being careful to leave wide bands of shrub and hedge between fields, creating a variety of habitats through mowing, digging ponds, and having no-trespass zones, where we leave everything as it is.

This has paid off even in the short time we have been here. Our bluebird population is amazing. Just last week, before the real cold hit, I saw six males on one fence, looking like bits of feathered sky.

The dogs luxuriate in all the room. I take them for several long walks a day, mostly around a safely fenced thirty acres close to the house. Julia, our German Shepherd female, who reigns supreme on Canterbury Farm, walks backward in front of me, stick in mouth, pleading with me to throw it, throw it. Sometimes I do. But she runs so hard and bounces so vigorously on her "prey" that several times a year she injures herself. Usually, it's as simple and painful as a ripped toenail. Though I try to be careful, past consequences never stop her from doing it again. I look for soft grassy areas to launch her into, for her own good and for my peace of mind.

Star, Julia's daughter and the owner of a large chunk of my heart, is off rodent hunting. She stands stock-still, tail stiff, ears arched forward, neck fully extended and alert. She listens; then, like in some movie of an Arctic fox, she springs into the air and lands front paws together on where she thinks the mouse is. Driving her nose into the grass, she frantically sniffs and digs. It's nice she has a hobby, even if she doesn't seem to be particularly successful at it.

Caras, our black-tri Australian Shepherd, who lives up to his family title of "World's Best Dog," is normally somewhere near, often leaping side to side in front of me. He is joyful to be outside with me. I would rather he simply walk, but the thrill of the moment frequently overcomes him. I can tell him to stop, but it makes me feel like such a scrooge that I put up with it.

Cedie, our small black ball of Australian Shepherd energy, is bouncing about, maybe chasing a bird, playing with Urs or seeking out some new disgusting thing to eat or roll in, or, best of all, roll in, *then* eat. She's the queen of all things gross.

Urs, our newly arrived German Shepherd male, is just thrilled to be free, in all this space. He romps off with the others, then circles back for a pat. Water is his thrill. He loves to wade, then drink and drink and drink. He becomes spectacularly dirty in an unbelievably short amount of time.

He treasures the drainage ditch that runs along our farm road under the fence and out to the highway in front. He wallows in the soft mud of the wet spot by the fence. He digs at the bottom, tossing gray clay-covered leaves everywhere. Diving in for unseen sticks in this mire, he pulls his face out—no longer black and red, it drips with murk. Finding a stick, he races off in glee, only to return to the puddle for more fun.

I have noticed through the years that dogs who have

spent months in a limited environment—such as a kennel or a pet shop—often don't know about the basics of life, such as stairs, vacuum cleaners, and to get out of the way of opening doors. Urs is no exception.

This day, his missing bit of learning has to do with the predictable effects of slippery surfaces plus momentum. With his bit of stick in his mouth, he races down the ditch, then spins, rear end low, head thrust forward, ears flat back, ecstatic to be alive. Racing back to the puddle, Urs leaps up, plants his front feet, lowers his head to bite the water, and slams skull-first into a fence post. It is a loud, dull thump. Urs stops for a second, shakes his head slightly, then races off again. This time when he returns, he gives himself plenty of room for his sliding stop. He's not dumb, just inexperienced.

Our family—canine, feline, ovine, equine, and human—never dreamed things could be this good. Our lives as trainers made this possible. For this, we thank all the jumping, barking, chewing, spinning, pulling, and in all other ways normal, if uncontrolled, canines everywhere. God bless you, each and every one!

Caribbean Husky (BRIAN)

That people have strong opinions about what breed they want is an understatement. People are dead set on the breeds they want and only the rare client will listen to our words of experience on the matter. So it was with the

Blacks. Their two Siberian Huskies had recently passed away and they wanted a new puppy. That in and of itself was fine—Siberians can be charming, and who was I to argue?

However, these people wanted the dog for Nassau—the island of Nassau, in the Bahamas. Why take a northern breed and stick it in a southern climate? But they were determined. Their last two had done well there, so why wouldn't this one? It was hard to argue with that, so I got them a beautiful silver Husky pup with blue eyes and a gray mask. Striking pup, outgoing and happy, as all good Siberians are.

The Blacks flew him down in their private plane; then several weeks later I arrived to start some basic training. Their main concern was a long pier jutting into an artificial canal where they moored their yacht. There was only one way out of the water if the pup took a tumble, and that was a set of stairs on the right side of the pier.

The first thing I did was put him on a snug buckle collar and leash. Then I slowly brought him up to the edge of the pier, keeping a firm hold of his collar lest he decide to jump. Most puppies have an instinctive fear of heights, and this one was no exception. He planted his sturdy little front legs and pulled back, saying, in every way a puppy can, No thank you! We went up to each side this way, until he gave the whole edge of the pier several feet of safety margin; then we walked around on a loose lead. He stayed well back from the edge.

That done, I stripped down to my swimsuit and carried him down the steps and into the water. Facing the steps, I gently lowered him into the warm canal. Holding him gently, I guided him to the stairs. He clambered out, shaking himself off. Looking offended by the whole process, he did not much care about the praise I heaped on his tiny shoulders. After a few minutes' rest, I repeated the process.

We practiced once or twice a day, until he could be placed anywhere within twenty feet of the steps and he would head straight back for them. He was not yet a graceful swimmer. Like most puppies, he made up for lack of style with energy. Eyes closed, nose skyward, he churned the blue waves with rapid front-leg scrambling. His rear end would sink; then he'd kick for a bit, and then it would sink again. I was glad I was there to help him learn. By the end of my visit, he was no Olympic swimmer, but he could get from point A to point B safely.

Other times throughout the day, we practiced puppy kindergarten, worked on housebreaking, and reviewed general manners. Housebreaking in the southern climes is a wonderful thing. Running a puppy out for a quick pee up north can entail coats, boots, mittens, hats, multiple doors, and so on. Here, it is simple: Puppy starts to sniff around; I run outside, clapping my hands and calling. Puppy follows. Then when we get to the designated place, I stand silent. He remembers what he was about to do, sniffs, urinates while I softly say, "Hurry up," and then we have a praise party afterward. What fun. Not only that; there are chameleons inside and out of the house to chase, endless birds to watch—how could life get better for a puppy?

Even the most wonderful puppy must rest, which left me time to relax. The Blacks and I went fishing on their forty-foot boat, gambling at local casinos, dining at walled-off country club communities, as well as indulging in the inevitable baking in the sun that doctors tell us not to do these days.

While all this was great fun for the first few days, the training was cut short by a family crisis. Mrs. Black found out that Mr. Black, her husband of several decades, had been supporting a second wife and several children in another country.

As you can imagine, Mrs. Black shared her rage, shock, confusion, and sadness with her spouse at full volume. Grabbing a book and the puppy, I retreated to my bedroom. Not that retreat helped much; the open layout of the house brought me every sob and every accusation in excruciating detail. I tried unsuccessfully to read. I ended up staring at the same page for minutes at a time. My tiny companion was oblivious, soundly asleep next to the bed, legs straight up in the air, head folded back in an impossible position. He had the right idea. After tucking him into his crate, I turned off the lights and willed myself to slumber. When I awoke, all was calm. I could hear quiet voices in the living room. Ice chinked in glasses. It must be cocktail hour, I thought.

I lay in bed for a time, trying to figure out what to say when I rejoined the group. "How was your afternoon?" "How is everyone?" Nothing seemed appropriate. Finally, I got up, slicked my hair back, and, deciding that even Emily Post would be challenged by this one, entered the fray, choosing the age-old approach of When you don't know what to say, pretend nothing happened. Everyone else took the same road. We spent the evening exchanging forced, tight-lipped smiles and horribly stilted conversation. The next day, I flew back to the relative calm and sanity of Manhattan.

HIS BITE IS WORSE THAN HIS BARK

Men Only! (BRIAN)

Even for a Bullmastiff, Brutus was a massive animal. A cross between a Bulldog and the huge ancient Mastiff breed, the Bullmastiff was created to hold a person in one place until the dog's owner arrived. Tipping the scales at over 165 dark brindle pounds of hard-packed muscle, Brutus was a stunning, if serious, dog.

His problem was unique. Owned by a Westchester doctor, Brutus was a sexually active dog whose preferences ran toward the human female and extreme privacy. If a woman entered his domain, he loped over with all the delicacy of a freight train, hopped on up, and started the canine rumba. If the woman was lucky, she was near a wall where she could brace herself. If unlucky, she was laid out flat and propelled across the floor with every thrust.

This was mortifying enough, but to make it worse, Brutus was not to be disturbed. Only two things stopped Brutus: the natural culmination of his activities or being interrupted. If anyone tried to stop him, he dismounted long enough to attack the gallant fool, then returned to his previous business.

From a trainer's point of view, there was one more important fact, possibly the most important fact: Brutus was attack-trained. His owner had a wide range of drugs in his office that he wanted kept safe, so Brutus had been professionally trained how to fight a human being successfully. This changed him from a big, intimidating dog to a big, intimidating dog with the equivalent of a black belt in karate. I don't care who you are; that many pounds of canine trained to do serious harm to a human body is nothing to trifle with. We all respected him a great deal and feared him more than a little. Hence, the sign on the door of his kennel read MEN ONLY!

Everyone in the kennel not only knew this story but had been warned by the boss to follow the rules to the letter. Why Debbie chose to tempt fate, I will never know. What I do know is that I was lying in the dorm above the kennels, reading. Latitia, the training director, was writing up some notes, and Steve, another trainee, was napping when we heard the screaming. We leapt up and ran down the worn wooden stairs. As we approached, the screaming took on a rhythmic quality, like a car trying to start on a cold day.

Reaching the bottom platform, we flung open the door and stopped midstride. Latitia, partially closing the door for our protection, gasped. Peering around the edge of the door, we took in the scene. Brutus was out of his cage and in the corridor. Debbie stood gripping the top of the kennels. These ran in two long banks down the kennel room, with a corridor in between. They were chain link and about four feet tall. She held on to the pipe running along the top of the chain-link panel. Grasping it with both hands, she was barely able to stay standing.

Debbie was a pear-shaped woman, which was causing a problem. Brutus chose a flank assault, gripping her just above her hip at her widest spot. As he got down to serious thrusts, he slid down her body. Releasing momentarily, he would grab up high again, only to slide back down. This process was removing her pull-on polyester pants. Needing both hands to stay standing, Debbie had no hand free to cover herself. This partial disrobing was mortifying for all of us, but the differences in the canine and human species ensured that there was no actual threat of consummation.

Slowly, Steve opened the door wider, easing himself partway into the kennel corridor. All canine motion stopped. Brutus froze, except for his eyeballs, which he rolled in Steve's direction. Up from the depths of his massive body rose a sound. It was the kind of savage growl that makes you shudder. Slowly, Steve slid back behind the door. He had been gone only a few seconds, but his forehead had broken out in sweat.

"Help me," Debbie begged. She was verging on tears. Brutus shoved his head against her shoulder. His growling had a definite beat.

Long silence from the stairs.

"Get him *off* me!" Her voice raised in frustration. Brutus stared almost eyeball-to-eyeball with the pale object of his desire. After a few seconds of silence, he proceeded.

The three of us looked at one another, then back at the

dog. "No way. Wait it out. You read the sign, didn't you?" We weren't volunteering to be mauled. Debbie, while mortified, was not being hurt. Anyway, this wouldn't take long. Dogs rival enthusiastic teenage boys in staying power, and while we were sure it lasted a lifetime for Debbie, it would in fact be just a minute or two at most.

When Brutus had finished, he slowly dismounted. He shook himself, then trotted into his kennel for a drink of water. He apparently had worked up quite a thirst. Debbie took the opportunity to slam the kennel door shut and beat a hasty retreat, hiking up her pants as she went.

No woman at that kennel ever gave Brutus such an opportunity again.

Horror (SARAH)

Pet therapy is one of the many wonderful gifts that animals and people give to one another. I have taken my dogs to nursing homes, schools, halfway houses, and institutions, where I have seen tiny miracles—if a miracle can ever be tiny. Everyone who does this work sees these types of miracles. My experience is not unique.

I have watched people who have long ago left this reality for a better one, then come back to ours for a visit when their eyes met a dog's. To see experienced nurses' mouths drop open when something they thought of as a "nice thing to do for the patients" brings coherent words and meaningful eye contact from a person they had not heard speak in many years is something you never forget. It taught me, yet again, never to underestimate the power of simple things to touch a person's heart.

But the story I tell here is not about such wonders. It's about trauma, something that should never happen in such a situation.

It happened on a fall day when I was participating in a visit to a school for the deaf in Manhattan. Kesl was with me, as he was my rock. He could handle anything, which is just what deaf children will give a dog. Of all the populations I have worked with, these youngsters are the biggest challenge. They are enthusiastic, active, engaged, fascinated, and ear-shatteringly loud. They cannot hear themselves, so when they squeal, scream, and yell in excitement, they are unaware of the impact they can have on a dog. Loud noises frighten many dogs. Others associate yelling with human anger. Kesl was his normal unflappable self, so I had no worries.

That day, we were in a small group, a Labrador, a Toy Poodle, a Springer Spaniel, and Kesl. Both the Springer's and the Poodle's handlers were new to this work, but they were catching on fast. The Labrador was owned by the group leader. Unusual for the breed, he had a tough streak in him that his handler did not always see coming.

After a couple of classroom visits, we all headed to the auditorium to do a presentation for the older children. As is my way, I went ahead, up the stairs to the stage. I could hear the doors opening behind me; the sound of excited children filled the room. As I turned my back, bending over

Kesl to pour him some water for a quick drink, I heard a scuffle of paws and a small human cry. Turning, I saw the owner of the Labrador pulling her dog back, the Poodle owner frozen, face a mask of horror, the tiny Poodle vomiting up a puddle of blood.

Moving across the stage, I just managed to scoop up the tiny limp animal in my arms as its legs buckled. Cradling him, I knew he was dead. His head lolled over my arm; gray tissue hung from his mouth in a thick strand.

The children, eyes wide with worry and surprise, stood in the aisle, halfway down to the stage. We could not have this scene here, not in front of the children. I grabbed the owner's arm with my free hand, spinning her firmly toward the group leader.

"We are going now." I started walking. "We have to go now." I did not want the kids to see this animal. His blood dripped onto my shoe. I supported his head a bit to make it look less gruesome. It might fool a few of the kids, though I doubted it. They miss very little.

Passing a teacher, I stopped. "We've had an accident here. Please close the curtain. I'll be back in a few minutes." Kesl trotted at my heel obediently. Outside the school doors, I downed him on the sidewalk. The group leader flagged the driver, who pulled the car around. "Go to your vet." I could have been wrong—anyway, it gave them all someplace to go. Whatever had to be discussed needed discussing away from this school.

"Is she . . ." the leader asked.

"I don't know," I responded, not quite truthfully, but

the owner was so pale, I did not want to upset her further. Anyway, what did I know? I'm no vet.

"Take her," I said, holding the dog out to the leader.

"I can't," she stated. Then she looked at the owner, who clearly couldn't and wouldn't be able to carry the shattered body of her tiny dog. She took the limp body. She adjusted the dog in her arms. Her chin set slightly. She knew the dog was dead and she knew that I knew. We said nothing. The leader ushered the owner into the car and off they went.

Alone on the sidewalk, I turned to the huge doors leading inside. My right hand, shirt, and shoes were spattered in blood. Calling Kesl to me, I unhooked the leash from around my waist and clipped him up. He didn't need it, but it wasn't good for the kids to see him off lead. As I leaned back, heaving the door open, I was met by the teacher I had spoken to in the auditorium. "What happened?" she asked.

"I don't know," I answered. "I didn't see, but I think his neck was broken." She gasped. "Where's the bathroom?" I asked, holding out my bloody hand.

"Oh my. Over here. It's the staff's."

"Good idea," I answered, not wanting to run into any children. Fortunately, I had worn a favorite dark floral-print shirt that day with dark slacks and dark shoes. Within minutes, no sign of the misery remained except for several wet spots on my clothes.

As I walked down to the stage, past those two hundred or so children, all eyes were riveted on me. Some of the older kids who spoke well asked me, "What happened? Did that big dog kill the little dog? Is the little dog dead?" I answered them as honestly and briefly as I could: "Don't know. Don't know." Then I ducked behind the curtain.

The pool of blood had expanded to its maximum. I scouted around for something to clean it up with. A pile of elementary school paper towels had been left for me. If you remember anything about those stiff, coarse towels, you remember that they don't absorb well. I couldn't really wipe up the blood; I sort of had to corral it from the sides, then scoop it up. Foul business, but I could not leave it for anyone at the school to do.

When I had it mostly cleaned up, I doused the area with a bit of Kesl's water. Swabbing up the last remnants took only seconds more. Going to the curtain, I opened it and began the talk on humane education.

Why did I do it? I could have left, I suppose, but I did not want these children's last memories of this event to be bad ones, or their last memories of dogs to be of violence, or the teachers' last thoughts about pet therapy and humane education to be negative. The work is too valuable, too important, to be jeopardized by one nightmarish incident.

Kesl was a ham and therefore a star. Who can resist a massive black fur ball who bounces with glee? We did our usual routine about pet care being a lot like infant care, the importance of spaying and neutering, how to approach a dog, how to prevent dogs from chasing you, and what to do if they do. Two children held up a broomstick for Kesl to jump over. Some of the kids read my lips, others watched the interpreter who signed off to one side, and a few, riveted on Kesl, did not seem to care what I was saying. By the end of the forty minutes, everyone was smiles, which was all I had hoped to accomplish.

The Gift (BRIAN)

When I started out in the business, I worked at few different kennels with different trainers before I met Barbara Woodhouse. In one of these first kennels, I helped train dogs for personal protection.

Though I enjoyed the work, I do not recommend this type of training. I have a simple rule to emphasize the difficulties: "If you can get your dog to sit, then I will train it for protection work." Many of you may be saying, "Well heck, my dog knows how to sit!" Oh? I mean when you open the door and the dog is halfway out, and you say, "Sit" —once— the dog sits without hesitation. I mean that while your dog is chasing a squirrel, you say, "Sit"—once—and the dog sits without hesitation. I mean that while he's eating his dinner, you say, "Sit"—once—and the dog stops eating and sits.

Now I can hear the complaints. "That's impossible!" you say. No it isn't. It is difficult, but not impossible. Stopping a highly agitated, aggressive dog during protection work is much more difficult. That situation demands a high level of control and a commitment to learning the skills required to manage such a dog. Teaching a dog to be aggressive is a serious business—not just from a control point of view but from a liability perspective, as well. Many insurance policies do not cover attack-trained animals.

Not only could this training cost a person his life, and cost you your home and peace of mind; an uncontrolled dog attack hurts the reputation of the animals I have devoted my life to helping. No client asking about this training has ever accomplished the level of "Sit" I require, so I have not done protection work for many years.

The fact is that an obedience-trained dog, one who sits quietly at your side when you open the front door, is plenty of intimidation for most situations. As much fear as our media generates about our society, most of us live peaceful lives in peaceful communities, with no pressing need for an omnipresent protection dog.

But back when I was learning dog training, the protection work was exciting and challenging. This story is about Rocco, a dog who taught me a great deal about training, ethics, and professional responsibility.

Rocco was a Doberman Pinscher from the era when Dobermans were not the delightful mush balls many of them are today. This was a fearful dog, selected by a dog-show handler for attack work on the basis that the dog flung himself savagely at the kennel gate whenever he saw a human being. This, the handler assessed, would make him a fine personal protection dog.

Nothing could be further from the truth. That kind of dog is as useful as a bodyguard who attacks everyone he sees. The best dogs for protection work are calm, well-socialized dogs who do not look for trouble but who have the courage to face it if it comes their way. They do not start fights; they finish them. The rest of the time, they lie quietly at their human's feet.

Rocco was not such a dog. He was fearful, reacting to his fear with aggression. Additionally, he had a problem with training. The problem was that if he was stimulated in any way—confusion, pain, fear, general excitement—he would instantly attack his handler.

This is a bad thing, especially if you are the one holding the leash. This ugly behavior is called "displacement aggression." In those years, at that kennel, this type of behavior was met with extreme force. Rocco received massive collar corrections, which stimulated him more, made him more fearful, and created more pain. So Rocco became more aggressive. It's like giving gas to an engine you are trying to turn off.

I came into the picture because no one would handle him but me. Frankly, no one could handle him but me. I understood his problem. As a child, I had been assaulted for years and understood too well Rocco's fear.

Not that Rocco was Rin Tin Tin with me. Not at all, but he was manageable—barely. I did not cause him pain or fear. I kept him moving, using enthusiastic praise to relax him. After his initial treatment during "training," he continued to expect the worst from humans, but made a small, tentative exception for me.

But he could not be agitated. Any type of protection work caused him to lash out at the closest thing to him—

me. The owner of the kennel tried everything he knew. The helper would step out and threaten Rocco. Rocco would instantly come for me. The helper would flank the dog (meaning, he would reach in *very* fast and pinch him in the soft flap of skin that drapes from the hind thigh to the belly). This created pain, and Rocco . . . well, you can imagine his response.

I asked to meet with the kennel owner in private and voiced my concerns about how this dog was unsafe and could not be made safe, that this client was coming to us in good faith and we were returning that faith with a dangerous dog. My boss, however, did not appreciate being told how to run his successful business by a novice trainer. The handler who selected the dog was too politically important to insult, the money involved too exorbitant—this dog was just fine.

The day the client came in his limousine to collect the dog, I did the only thing I could think of doing. I gift wrapped a box of Band-Aids and handed it to the bodyguard. He unwrapped them and looked at me questioningly.

"What are these for?"

"You'll see," I said.

Within weeks, the inevitable happened. In Chicago, two young thugs attempted to get into the limo. The bodyguard gave the command to attack. Rocco looked at the young thugs, leapt from the front seat into the back, and launched himself at the unfortunate bodyguard. This man, though trained to handle violent humans, was in no way prepared for this close-quarters canine assault.

Rocco must have looked something like a mountain

lion in a fish bowl. The young thugs, duly intimidated, ran away. The bodyguard suffered multiple wounds, requiring ninety-some stitches to close. Band-Aids were not enough.

A Little Problem (SARAH)

As my grandmother always said, "No good deed goes unpunished." And so it was with Janice and her dog, Freeway. Janice called in a panic. "Please take Freeway. Please. I am going on my honeymoon, and I don't want to worry about him. Please. Mrs. Williams gave me your number."

We don't normally take dogs we haven't trained. This policy ensures that the dogs are more relaxed, since they know us, and this lessens stress-related barking, fasting, or depression. But this was an emergency and the Williamses were good clients, so I bent the rules.

Janice, incredibly grateful, brought Freeway up the next weekend. Out of her Audi popped an adorable older black American Cocker Spaniel. Clearly just back from his groomer, he had a red ribbon on each ear. That probably was the groomer's subtle signal to me to look out. In the world of horses, a red ribbon on the tail means the horse kicks. But I did not pause.

Freeway, nine, had been found seven years ago on a major highway—thus, his name.

"What do I need to know about him?" I asked.

"Oh, nothing; he's just a doll." She bent over and stroked him in quick short strokes.

After interviewing her on his diet, general health, vaccination history, and favorite pastimes (such as chewing bones, playing with other dogs, chasing a ball—Freeway had none), I popped him into his crate and waved good-bye to Janice. I felt pleased that I had made an exception. She was a lovely woman and he seemed like a happy little dog. Sometimes the rules need to be bent.

The first crack in that perfect picture appeared when I next interacted with Freeway. I noticed a horrible stench coming out of his mouth. I put him up on the grooming table and opened his mouth for a peek. I had never and to this day have never seen anything like what greeted me. He had tartar so thick that it came out past gumline. Those gums were receded a half inch or more in places. The teeth themselves were clearly compromised.

Any vet would have seen this mess and suggested cleaning long ago. Any loving owner would not have ignored it to this disgusting and no doubt painful point. Janice had dropped off a squeeze bottle of flavored mouthwash. Now I understood why. But that was like using a Dixie cup to bail out a sinking ship. I made a large note on her chart to discuss it with her in two weeks when Freeway was picked up. There was nothing to be done about it now. This would require major surgery to rectify.

The first few days were uneventful. He was a nice-enough boarder. Kept to himself some. Didn't want a lot to do with me, but that isn't so unusual in an older dog who lives an ordinarily indulged life.

As the days went by, we gave him more freedoms. He could trot in and out without being on a lead. He could hang out with us in the grooming room as we did laundry or paperwork—the normal stuff.

One evening, I let him out of his crate to go outside, and he took a side trip to put his nose in one of the larger kennels. There was a food bowl in there, apparently with a good smell still on it. "Freeway, come on, boy," I called, standing by the door to the outside runs. "Come on."

No sign of recognition. "Piglet," I muttered as I walked across the floor. "Come on, fella," I said again, bending down and patting him affectionately on the butt. "You already ate."

All I saw coming at me was nasty mossy teeth against black, black fur. If Dr. Jekyll had put his head into the crate, Mr. Hyde came out. There I was, in shorts. Every muscle in my legs tightened. It felt as if I'd sucked my kneecaps behind my knees. I scrambled backward. Freeway was running in place. The tile floor and his fuzzy Cocker feet gave him poor traction. If not for that fluke of fate, I'd be showing you my scars about now.

The wall came up all too soon and Freeway was beginning to make some headway. Pressed against the wall, on my tiptoes, I had no place to go. As he got to me, I took the towel I had over my shoulder and swung it back and forth in front of me in an effort to deter him. It was the only defense I could come up with on such stunningly short notice. I did not swing it at him. I knew that any act of aggression on my part would only make him worse. Within a few seconds, he subsided. He stared at me for a moment or two, then, having made his point perfectly clear, returned to licking the bowl clean.

I let him.

After he was done, I called him out the door as usual, as if nothing had happened. He trotted out. He never was off lead again.

When I mentioned this to Janice later, her response was "Oh, yes. Did we forget to tell you? He has a little problem around food."

King of the West Side (BRIAN)

When I met King, a Border Collie/Chow mix, he was just a ball of nine-week-old fuzz. Frank, his owner, boasted that the day he got King from the shelter, he stopped at a bar on the way home. When a friend went to get something out of Frank's truck, seven-week-old King wouldn't let him in.

I had problems with most of this story. Who leaves a pup you have just picked up alone? Who leaves a pup loose in a car, at any time? Who leaves a pup to go to a bar? Who lets anyone open the door with a loose pup in the car? Who takes such pride in a young pup's aggression?

None of this was promising, but Frank was eager and could use some help. King was a puppy more than capable of surviving much mishandling, but the question was: Would everyone else?

When I arrived, the apartment was filled with people. The family unit itself—wife, father, assorted kids—curious neighbors, and a few extended family members were there to observe. This occasionally happens. Calling in a professional dog trainer is a novelty to many people. I heard lots of "I've had dogs all my life, but I never needed a dog trainer." To which I always yearn to respond, "I've been around cars all my life, but I still don't know how to fix one." But I don't. I just say how lucky they are to have had such nice dogs that they never needed any help with them.

Within minutes of my arrival, they showed off King's newest and favorite game. It involved giving him a big chunk of meat. King would grab it, stand for a moment or two in quiet contemplation, trot to the center of the room, drop the meat, stand over it for a second or two more, then trot off by the sofa to lie down with feigned indifference.

This in and of itself scared the hell out of me. For any dog, never mind a rapidly growing pup, to forgo meat for some reason, any reason, showed either a level of overfeeding that was not evidenced in his build or a level of thought that I don't like to see in pups of the powerful breeds, especially ones owned by novices with bulging macho streaks.

After a minute or two, a person walked into the middle of the room and casually reached for the meat. Out King flew from his sideline position. Standing over his prize, he snarled and snapped savagely. The person wisely retreated. King stood there for a moment or two longer, then retired to his lookout spot, leaving the meat behind.

Even Frank was a bit wide-eyed at this. He looked at me half with pride and half with concern. I supported the concern.

"This is *very* serious behavior at any age, in any breed,"

I began. "But in a young puppy . . ." I shook my head slightly. "You need to get serious about his training today and"—I looked Frank straight in the eye—"you need to stop supporting his aggression. No more rough play. No more laughing when he is aggressive. I cannot say this strongly enough. You will never have a problem with this pup being cowardly. You will have problems with him biting you, your children, and your friends if you don't act right now. Even then, I can't make you any promises."

Frank nodded. He stared at the pup with a slight frown. "Yeah, I know. That's why I called you. I like him a bunch."

"He's one smart puppy," I responded. If I had been completely truthful, I would have said, "He's too smart for the average household." Superior intelligence can be a real drawback in most homes.

Honey, Help? (SARAH)

I met Jango, a five-year-old male Kuvasz, in the late eighties, shortly after Brian and I started living together. Jango was a regular with Brian for boarding, as well as a frequent training guest. These stays entailed either flying him up from his home in Maryland or having the chauffeur make a special trip, but Jango's owner wanted the best for her dog. Besides, no place else would take him.

He and Brian were old friends, but he and I had our own relationship to work out. We had been doing fine together. While I wouldn't have called us buddies, I thought we were beginning to get used to each other. He scared me a bit with his intensity, size, and reputation for being more than just talk, but I liked him. It was hard not to. He strolled the planet as if he owned it and had never met a person or dog who had convinced him otherwise. He threw down his canine gauntlet with me in the early hours of one Saturday morning.

I have no recollection of where our house dogs were that morning, but I do clearly recall waking up bleary-eyed in the dark and padding off to the bathroom. I noted, casually, that Jango was asleep in a heap, next to Brian's side of the bed. Fine.

I did not bother with a robe and, as is my habit, was wearing just a T-shirt. I only share this detail with you so you get the full impact of my return, still half-asleep, turning the corner back into the bedroom, only to meet the bared teeth of a serious dog. Not that he bothered standing up to threaten me—no, that would have been too much effort. He had taken the tactically fully defensible position of lying in the doorway. In fact, he spilled over a bit on either side. He lay here, head on the floor, eyes like brown laser beams, lips fully raised. His intentions were clear: I was not reentering the bedroom. He did not move; neither did I.

Every hair on my body stood on end. Goose pimples raised on parts of me that, prior to this moment, had never had goose pimples. I stood, a deer in the headlights. This dog was good at what he did—very good.

"Come on, Jango," I said halfheartedly, turning as if to walk away, patting my bare leg invitingly. "Come *on,* boy. That's a good boy. Let's go for a walk." I clapped my hands merrily.

It was a pathetic attempt. Jango did not even blink. I thought about becoming verbally tough, but that seemed like a potentially incredibly stupid thing to do. I mean, don't dial a number that you don't want answered. Jango had already demonstrated at home a willingness to follow through on his threats. I did not wish to be another notch on his collar.

I then made an attempt to waken Brian. It might have been easier to move Jango. Brian sleeping defines the expression "to sleep like the dead." "Brian," I whispered. "Ah, Brian, you awake?" Stupid question. His even breathing gave me my answer. "Brian," I said again, a little louder. Jango raised his head, leaning forward ever so slightly. He did not approve.

Leaning a bit forward from my waist, I tried once more. "Brian, I need you!" Covers flew aside and Brian sat bolt upright, searching right and then left for the emergency. Involuntarily, I stepped back. Wow, those were clearly the magic words.

"What—" he began to say, then saw the dog. "Jango," he chided.

The beast rose, trotting to Brian with ears back, head lowered, plumed tail waving merrily from side to side. "Place," Brian told him. Jango curled back down on his spot. As this was going on, I scurried back to bed, diving under the covers for warmth. "What'ya say we start crating him at night?" I ventured.

"Uh-huh," Brian replied as he fell back instantly into a sound sleep.

Why call the dog? Why not correct him? Because first

of all, he was doing his duty. He didn't lunge or snap; he simply stood his ground. This was part of Jango's job back home, a job he did well. Secondly, it isn't a good idea to correct a dog like Jango without a lead and collar and a tactical advantage. Jango simply did not intimidate. You had to impress this animal with your intelligence, and the most intelligent thing to do at that moment was to offer him an easy way out and have him take it. I lay in bed thinking about that lesson as I drifted back to sleep. I dreamed of being eaten by white lions. Wonder what that meant?

Can Leap Tall Fences in a Single Bound (SARAH)

No one was home when I pulled up to our house. I had been away for a few days. The kennel was full, mostly with dogs I knew well. As I walked through the kennel for a quick check of the animals before I headed upstairs, a telltale smell hit me. Someone had dirtied their crate. Of course, because I had just driven eight hundred miles in a day and a half and was stiff from sitting so long, it had to be the large Golden Retriever/Great Pyrenees mix I'd never laid eyes on before. When I bent down to look into her crate, she urinated.

"Great. Perfect." I took a minute to check the boards. No warnings were posted to keep this dog, Mable, on a lead or to watch her around our other animals, so I opened the crate door, ushering her into an outdoor pen. She scooted through the pen's gate, head and tail down, slinking swiftly to the rear of the run. Turning, she looked up at me from her crouched position. The whites of her eyes showed. Oh, *this* is going to be fun! I said to myself before turning back to the kennel.

A roll of paper towels and ten minutes spent with a scrub brush later, I pulled my head out of the now-spotless crate. As I pulled off the rubber gloves, I peered out the window at Mable. She was pacing the rear of the pen like a cornered lioness. Lithe, muscular, weighing in at somewhere over one hundred pounds, this was a dog to respect.

I gathered up some dog biscuits. I had no real confidence that she would take them, but you never know. Most truly frightened animals won't eat, but I thought it would be a delightfully easy solution if she would. Grabbing a lead as well, I started talking as I approached the run. When she saw me come out of the house, she froze, half-crouched, watching me approach. As I got to the gate, I paused, continuing to talk to her gently. I swung the gate open, then stepped aside. My goal was to get her back inside before trying to get my hands on her. We did not share that goal. She remained frozen, staring at me as if I were a serial killer and she were next in line.

I stepped into the neighboring run, hoping to move down one side, thereby urging her out the front gate of her pen. Again, we saw things differently. As I walked down the run, she reared up her full five-foot-plus height. Pivoting in place, she pressed herself into the far corner, scrambling for all she was worth. She was up and over the fence in a heartbeat, racing off down the runway between our chain-link runs and stockade fence.

My jaw swung open as I watched her bolt around the corner. Oh, this is so ugly, I thought. Retrieving a panicked dog is a dangerous business at any time. Retrieving a panicked dog when you are home alone is dangerous and stupid. Retrieving a panicked Great Pyr mix who is now cornered in a narrow alleyway between two fences while home alone was beyond dangerous and stupid; it was insane, but there was no other option.

As I stood pondering this mess, I heard a crash. Running to the corner of the house, I saw that Mable had blown right through the chain link at the end of the alleyway, ripping it away from the stockade it was nailed to. She probably had not even seen it in her panic. She was now running loose in our fenced side yard—a side yard fenced on two sides with a six-foot stockade but on the other two with four-foot chain link. This just kept getting worse.

I raced back through the kennel room, into the garage, threw open the door, grabbed my shepherd's crook, which had heretofore been reserved for working with my sheep, and sprinted into the side yard. Flinging open the large gate into the pen behind the house, I assessed the situation. Then, doing my best Border Collie imitation, I did a wideout run to my left along the chain-link fence. As I arced out, she turned back toward the stockade, as any frightened sheep would.

I steadied up and came along the back fence line, maneuvering her toward the house. She ran away from me toward the open gate. Excellent! I could herd her one pen at a time back into the kennel room.

Just as she went to run through the gate, she veered off into a corner. Here the chain link was a little taller, but I had just seen her climb like a monkey. If I waited, I would give her time to think. I did not want her to think. Veering back into the yard, I moved toward her fast. I slapped the chain link with the crook, hoping to frighten her away from the fence. I did not want to add to her fear, but I saw few options. I had to move her. I opted for making her leery of the fence and the crook and tried to keep myself out of it as much as I could—no shouting, no lurching at her. The fence slap worked, but now I had a large, terrified dog staring right at me. I slowed. "Easy, girl. Easy. We just need to go back into the kennel." I couldn't allow her to turn back to the fence, but I didn't want to force her into aggression, either. I halted about ten feet from her. Standing ready to slap the fence again if she turned, I gave both of us a minute to settle down. After that, I had to take some action.

Slowly taking the wrong end of the crook in my hand, I slid the hook along the ground toward her. Standing sideways, hunching over, I tried to appear as unthreatening as possible. She pulled back away from the approaching hook but had nowhere to go.

Quickly, I slid the hook of the crook up, under her neck, and into her buckle collar. Luck smiled, and I had her. She spun out to the side, pulling back, bucking like a rodeo bull. She dragged me with her. "Whoa, Mable. Whoa, big girl." I reverted to horse talk, since her power reminded me of those days. I prayed she wouldn't come at me. The shepherd's crook worked well for pressure away from me, but if she came at me, she'd slide right up the smooth wood. I would have little defense.

Thankfully, she elected to spin in circles around me, and as long as I stood like a rock in the center, holding on for dear life, we were fine.

After spinning around for a minute or two, Mable crouched into a shivering pile. "Let's go into the kennel," I said happily, trying to set a positive tone. "Let's go, girl." I gave her a gentle tug. Leaping forward, she dragged me toward the house, into the kennel room, then dove into her crate. With a huge sigh, I closed the door on the crook and braced myself against the door. She was not going to make a break for it this time. Unhooking the crook, I latched the crate door. "Good girl, Mable. Good girl," I said. She was not interested in my congratulations.

Remembering the biscuits in my pocket, I shoved them through the bars. She didn't even look at them. With a few more kind words, I left for a shower, a warm cup of tea, and a well-deserved sit-down. Later, when I came down, the biscuits were gone. That, at least, was a start.

CROSSING THE LINE

Wet Dreams (SARAH)

Pal and his owner, Ruth, lived in large brick building on a pretty street in Brooklyn. Wild barking met my knock on the door. The noise got louder, then softer, louder, then softer. Either he was coming forward, then backing away—a sign of lack of confidence—or he could have been running back and forth between his owner and the door. I couldn't tell.

Ruth's voice was gentle and sweet. "Pal, sit. Sit down, Pal. Pal, please sit." This was clearly the right apartment. Pal's barking continued unabated. Ruth cracked open the door. "Sarah?" she asked.

"Yes, hello, you must be Ruth. You sound like you have your hands full," I said, smiling at her. She rolled her eyes.

"Yes, just a second." Her face disappeared. A moment later, the door swung open. The first thing I saw was Ruth leaning back like a water-skier, both hands on the collar of her enthusiastic Dalmatian, as Pal leapt a happy greeting.

"What a handsome dog," I began. It never hurts to pay a sincere compliment to a client's dog. Sincerity is the key, as both people and dogs can pick out a fake.

I could see that for all of Pal's lunging, it was enthusiasm, not aggression, we were dealing with. "Do you have his leash handy?" I asked.

"Oh, yes, of course. I'm terribly sorry." Ruth was a very sweet woman, but getting her to do the kind of asserting necessary to get control of this bundle of boundless energy might be a challenge.

Once Pal was on the lead, we were able to do a quick session on "Off" and "Leave it." This calmed Pal down enough for me to interview Ruth reasonably uninterrupted. I do an extensive phone interview, but new issues often arise once I am in the home.

The apartment was spotless, if a bit sparse. The TV was probably born about the same year I was. Everything matched, a warm rose being the primary color. Several pictures of landscapes dotted the walls, along with a few portraits of Jesus. A cross hung over the television.

Being deeply religious occasionally influences the relationship between the dog and the human, especially, we have found, with some women. We have noticed that these rare women have three similarities: They are single, they are devout, and their religion links sex with sin. Ruth fit the bill perfectly, though it is with hindsight I am telling you this. At the time, I missed the telltale signs completely.

Pal's presenting problem was a strong aggressive reaction to machine noise. He was fine on the street, but indoors, he was a maniac. He had already eaten several vacuum hoses. If Ruth used the blender, Pal spun in place, barking nonstop. She used an electric razor to shave her legs, which sent Pal into such a frenzy that she had to lock herself in the bedroom to do the job. This made shaving possible, but it was clear from the deep scratch marks on the door that this system wasn't going to work forever.

Initially, when Pal was a pup, she had found these behaviors cute. As he grew into adolescence, they became a signature of his unique personality, then at adulthood, weighing in at a bold sixty-eight pounds, they became a real problem.

As is normal, I reviewed our phone interview to make sure I had all the facts straight. All went along well until an inner flag went up when we discussed sleeping arrangements. Pal was relegated to the hall outside her bedroom. This struck me as odd, not because that isn't a perfectly normal place for a dog to sleep but because during the whole twenty-minute conversation up to this point, she had not taken her hands off the dog. He leaned against her, obviously both used to and enjoying the attention. His mouth was open and relaxed, a blissful doggy grin.

When she reported the sleeping in the hall, I looked at her questioningly. "That's okay, isn't it?" she asked worriedly.

"Oh, yes, fine. It just surprised me a bit, since you seem very attached to each other. Does his shedding bother you?" Dalmatians are notoriously heavy shedders.

"No." She averted her eyes. "This is a little embarrassing," she said, hesitating.

"Believe me," I reassured her, "I've dealt with just about every dog behavior known to man, not to worry."

"Well, he was making number one on the pillow." She met my eyes briefly.

"Ah . . . do you use more than one pillow?" I was trying to be discreet. She was clearly uneasy, and why not?

"No, he makes on the pillow when I'm sleeping on it."

"Yuck, that can't be fun!"

"No, it isn't." She spoke more firmly. "That's why I put him in the hall."

It turned out that Ruth was a naturally gifted handler, despite my earlier concerns. Her devotion to her dog inspired determination. While I worried about how sweet Ruth was, I shouldn't have. She was more than up to the task of controlling Pal once she understood a few of the skills and theories necessary for her to be effective.

She stopped petting him all the time, which was causing him to think too highly of himself. In the world of dogs, he who doles out attention freely without asking for anything in return is, by definition, subordinate. Instead, she started ignoring him more, waiting for him to come to her for interaction. When he arrived, she made him do a command before petting him. She petted him briefly, leaving him wanting more of her attention. "Down" became an important command that she used liberally throughout her day. She controlled his jumping, taught him to allow her through doorways first, and soon could even make him stay when the vacuum was turned on—a victory I had not expected her to achieve so quickly.

But, with all the steady improvement, we still were having the pillow-peeing problem. While locking him out of the bedroom was 100 percent effective, if Ruth left the door ajar, she still awoke to early-morning showers. The impetus of his behavior puzzled me. What was going on?

I pondered this between sessions. Toward the end of our next meeting, when Ruth was jotting down her homework assignment, Pal gave me a positively intimate long, slow, lick on the arm—I pulled away. He pursued. I downed him, which he did. As I wiped my arm on my sweatshirt, I turned to Ruth.

"Ah, Ruth. That's a pretty intense lick. Is that normal for him?" I sounded as casual as I could.

She glanced up from her note taking. "Oh, yes." She smiled. "He loves to lick." She went back to her writing.

"When does he do this licking?" Again, I sounded casual, very casual.

"After my shower. I let him lick me dry." She smiled.

"Ah . . ." She did not think anything of this. As difficult as it might be to fathom, this was not sexual to Ruth. In her world, sex had a narrow definition and it did not include canine licking. To her, it was a completely innocent behavior. However, Pal did not find it so benign. "That may be the root of our problems here." It was *definitely* the root of our problems here! "I suggest we stop this ASAP." She looked at me questioningly. "Just keep him out of the bathroom when you are drying yourself, okay?"

"Okay," she said in a perfectly polite "if you say so" tone. Bless her, as with everything else I recommended, she followed through exactly. Success.

Cadet (SARAH)

Early on in Brian's and my relationship, we went to the home of a lovely woman who was having a problem with her large Collie/Lab cross. He was mounting her.

The building she lived in was typical of upper-middle-class apartment buildings in the city—big square stone on a street lined with big square stone buildings. They may all have started out some unique colors, but the city grime long ago brought them all to a common dingy gray.

The doorman called her from the foyer, then allowed us up. The day had been rainy, so the building staff had put runners down over the slick faux marble flooring. The elevator didn't keep us waiting long, so we got up to her fourth-floor apartment quickly.

When she swung open the door with a slight flourish, I immediately felt inadequate. Joanne was one of those women who knows how to pull together a look. She could no more wear a mismatched ensemble than the Pope could swear. A look is something I have never mastered on a day-to-day level. In fact, I have a gift for stains. The more I like an outfit, the more likely it is to be damaged within hours of putting it on. Joanne was one of those infuriating women who could wear silk to a barbecue and come out spot-free. I, on the other hand, could wear Kevlar to the library and arrive home ripped and smudged.

That day, she was dressed in tight head-to-toe black: black angora sweater with slightly poofy short sleeves, black leggings, followed by black pumps with three-inch heels, which she walked in as if she were barefoot. All of this was highlighted by a pair of tasteful gold earrings, a gold locket that hung down on a chain, emphasizing her impressive cleavage, gold bangle bracelets, and a thin gold chain belt.

Her apartment was equally carefully coiffed. A shiny black grand piano graced one wall, with the predictable line-up of flattering photos of Joanne and her loved ones taken in various exotic places. Her furniture was softly inviting. A comfortable-looking U-shaped black leather couch was the main piece. She even had the bold confidence to put down plush white wall-to-wall carpet, carpet one of my animals would have rolled on, vomited on, or otherwise stained before the door closed behind the installer.

Her dog, Cadet, not surprisingly solid black, greeted us with painful enthusiasm, if not control. After a few moments of claw-raking canine greeting involving full body contact in areas that I prefer not to be greeted in, Brian clipped a lead on him and taught him "Off." It only took a minute or two of praise-filled but no-nonsense teaching for Cadet to learn to control himself. Joanne was suitably impressed. Both of them looked at Brian rather adoringly as we all sat down to discuss Cadet's behavior.

Sitting facing Brian on the black leather couch, I watched him interview Joanne. Occasionally, he stroked Cadet's head as the dog sat pressed up against his leg.

Cadet had been adopted at around six months of age from a local shelter. He was Joanne's second dog, the first one being the apple of her eye. Silver-framed pictures of the first dog—a Golden Retriever mix—were proudly displayed on a nearby bookshelf. To hear her tell it, the dog was a saint. Maybe he was, and maybe he wasn't. The human memory is not reliable in this area.

Cadet was neutered and otherwise healthy. His pulling when on the lead, jumping up, and general rambunctiousness were completely normal for an untrained young dog. Now that Brian had a general background, he got down to the nitty-gritty.

"When is he mounting you?" he asked.

"When I play with him," Joanne answered. "It all goes along fine until he just—let me show you." With that, Joanne stood up, gave her angora sweater a downward tug, then lowered herself onto the plush carpet. On hands and knees, spiked heels pointing skyward, she proceeded to crawl along the floor, calling her dog.

Cadet pranced sideways, riveted on his owner. His raised tail waved back and forth like a flag. As he approached, she lowered her shoulders, raised her rump in the air, and, while wagging it back and forth, chanted his name. "Cadet . . . come here, boy. Where's Mommy's boy?" Cadet did a series of play bows, lowering his front end while raising his rear. He mimicked Joanne's posture almost exactly. Then he spun away, barked, then approached again.

I don't know whose eyes were wider, Brian's or mine. We stared at her for a moment, then at the dog, then at each other. If I had made a long list of the possible reasons for Cadet's behavior, this would not have been anywhere on it. I suddenly felt much less intimidated by this woman.

"Joanne!" Brian began curtly, clearly not amused by this floor show. She was quite involved with getting her dog's attention. A frown formed on Brian's face.

"Cadet, Cadet, Cadet," Joanne chanted, swaying her rear. "Come play with Mommy."

"Joanne! Get up," Brian demanded.

Joanne paused. "He's not going to. He always does. He must be shy around you."

"Get up!" Brian retorted. "I see where Cadet is getting confused." I've seen Brian stop all conversation in a restaurant using that particular tone. It's not loud. It's not angry. It is very serious. Joanne rocked back onto her knees.

"You do?" She was surprised. She rose daintily, brushing the pale carpet fibers from her knees. Cocking her head to one side like an eager Spaniel, she asked, "Can you stop him?"

"No, but *you* can—easily."

"Really!" She almost clapped her hands in excitement. "What do I need to do?"

"Simple, Joanne. Don't do that!" Stifling a laugh, I excused myself to use the powder room. When I rejoined the session, Brian had Joanne standing up, working Cadet. Staying vertical was the beginning of a cure.

Small But Mighty (BRIAN)

People who have never been faced with an aggressive small dog ask how such dogs can be intimidating. I always reply, "Would you be intimidated by a rat running across the room snapping its jaws at you?"

A small dog who is mentally and physically committed to doing you bodily harm can set most anyone back. That doesn't mean that some of the situations themselves aren't comical. So it was with John, his wife, and their four-pound black Poodle named Snickers.

John was a truck driver, a huge, fit man over six feet tall and carrying some two hundred muscled pounds. While an intimidating physical presence, he was an extremely nice man.

Being a truck driver, he was gone a great deal. In his absence his wife showered all her attention on the little dog. Also, being alone and sometimes a bit frightened at night, she encouraged Snickers to bark. Petting and praise were heaped on his little shoulders with every ferocious yip. She thought his efforts to protect the house "adorable."

So the stage was set. Enter John. Home from a long trip, exhausted, missing his wife in more than one way, he showers, brushes his teeth, goes into the bedroom, and reaches for the blanket so he can climb into his own bed at last. Snickers explodes—barking out of control, leaping straight up and down off the bed, snapping at him. John pulls back. "Jesus . . . What the hell . . ." His wife grabs Snickers. "Calm down, Punkin'. . . . It's just Daddy." She strokes the woolly tyrant soothingly. Snickers, encouraged by her praise, continues to growl, lifting his lips into a snarl. "I'll hold him, hon. You get into bed, he'll calm down. He's just being Mommy's little protector." She hugs the little dog close. The dog's eyes never leave John's face.

Frankly, John would like to reprimand the dog firmly, but he knows if he does so, his wife will be upset, which will ruin any hope of conjugal reunion. Cautiously, John climbs into bed. Snickers squirms left, struggles right, and is out of her hands. John swings his legs out of the bed for a hasty retreat. As the tiny hellion leaps at him, John stretches out a hand in self-defense. Snickers latches onto his index finger like a barnacle on a boat. John shakes his hand hard, splattering blood on the bedspread and the walls. Snickers flips back and forth in the air but hangs on relentlessly, making any terrier proud. John's wife is screaming, "You're hurting him! Don't hurt him!" She is referring to Snickers.

Finally, Snickers flies free, landing safely on the bed. Beth immediately scoops him up, holding him to her breast. "It's okay, Punkin'. Daddy didn't mean it!" John stares at this scene. "Oh, yes, Daddy did mean it," he states, ripping the blanket off the bed as he heads for the couch. At least there he can sleep in peace.

The next day, I got a call. Snickers came under control fairly quickly, once we got Beth straightened out. That took some talking on my part and I am sure a great deal of talking between husband and wife, but they came to an understanding—husband first, dog second.

Aggression rarely is easily dealt with, but in this case, it was a learned behavior, more than a part of the dog's basic temperament. Once Beth saw how she had been inadvertently training the dog to be aggressive by praising him every time he was, things moved along quickly. John took over all feeding, walking, and grooming routines. His wife ignored the dog 99 percent of the time, giving him attention only when he obeyed commands. Snickers was on house arrest, dragging a thin lead when he was loose with them, and crated when they could not supervise him carefully. He lost all furniture privileges, including the bed. All aggression, of any kind, was met by immediate disapproval from both John and Beth. A typical Poodle, he learned the new rules quickly. Certain things, like a relaxed version of house arrest, had to be maintained for his lifetime, but with management, he became an acceptably well-behaved member of the family within a matter of weeks.

A Definite Yes (SARAH)

Sarah, I'm so worried." Lisa sounded urgent.

"What's wrong?" I knew this client well, and she was not prone to unnecessary worry. She owned a Lhasa Apso, aptly named Fang. While not a name I would normally endorse, in this case, it was fair warning. Fang loved whom he loved. If you were part of his inner circle, he was charming, playful, and comical. If you were a stranger, he was none of those things.

I was lucky enough to be counted as a friend. For years, I had been urging Lisa to neuter Fang for health as well as attitude reasons. She had steadfastly refused. I hoped this was nothing too serious.

"Well, as I was cooking dinner, I noticed Fang wasn't in the kitchen. He always watches me cook. I went to find him, and he was standing in the hall—"

"Is he okay?" I interrupted.

"I don't know. He was just standing there hunched over, and there was a pool of liquid under him. He looked a little glazed, but . . . he's fine now."

"Ah, Lisa. Was it urine on the floor?"

"No. It's kind of cloudy, whitish. Did he have a seizure?" she asked.

"I don't think so, but check with your vet," I replied. "I'm betting he just, well, masturbated."

"Dogs can do that!" She was shocked.

"Some dogs can, and when they can, they do. Sounds like Fang just did."

"Will he do it again?"

"Lisa," I said, chortling. "I can guarantee you he will do it again. It is, shall we say, a self-rewarding activity."

"Oh. . . ." There was a pause as Lisa comprehended what I had said. "Can I stop him?"

"Yup, get him neutered."

When she did, then he didn't.

Don't Touch His Wooby (BRIAN)

The apartment was sophisticated, professionally decorated with soft, elegant peach tones and gloriously plush antiques. Piles of needlepoint pillows erupted from all possible corners of couches and chairs. Chintz curtains hung in floral waterfalls of fabric from the top of the ceiling-high windows down, forming puddles of color on the floor below. Oil paintings of English countryside and elegant rural scenes dotted the walls. And everywhere, on every surface, stood little baubles—china ashtrays, adorable statues of begging dogs, vases brimming with silk flowers. The whole thing was *House & Garden* goes overboard.

Dexter, a young male Fox Terrier groomed to perfection and sporting a spotless tan leather collar with shiny brass hardware, appeared to have stepped straight out of one of their paintings. His owners, Mr. and Mrs. Lowell, were describing the problems they were experiencing. "Dexter doesn't listen to us," Mrs. Lowell complained, leaning forward slightly on the couch, clasping her ring-bedecked hands together on her knees. "He doesn't even seem to hear us!" Her husband nodded his agreement. As she went on, Dexter trotted across the room, grabbed a cushion that lay on the floor, and enthusiastically humped it. How attractive, I thought.

"Excuse me," I interjected, "but—" I pointed to the dog.

"Oh, that's his Wooby," Mrs. Lowell explained. "He adores his Wooby."

"Clearly," I replied. Dexter was reaching a fevered pitch. "That is rather . . . unseemly."

Mr. Lowell smiled. "He's done that his whole life, even as a very small puppy. It's perfectly natural."

"Natural—okay, lots of things are natural, but that doesn't necessarily mean it's good for the dog's attitude or that it's something you want in your living room. Anyway, this is disgusting." I could see that this wasn't making the impression I needed. "What would you think if I started to behave this way in your living room? It's natural. . . ." I let my voice trail off. The Lowells drew back in unison. Bingo! Got their attention.

"Ah-h-h," Mr. Lowell said. Nodding gravely but then shrugging, he looked toward his distracted pet. "There's not much we can do about it. He won't let anyone touch his Wooby."

"Touch it!" I exclaimed as I watched the dog dismount from his love-dampened object of obsession. "Who would want to touch it?"

After surreptitious Wooby removal, neutering, structure, and increased exercise, Dexter became less sexually crazed, though I wouldn't ever have called him obedient.

Pardon Me? (SARAH)

Not many clients fluster me. We deal with a full range of people in our profession, and I am well used to the rich and famous. But not *this* rich and *this* famous. This person was kind enough to invite us to join him for dinner. Over dessert, he asked about a behavior his large male German Shepherd was indulging in that was troubling him. "Connor likes to drag his rear, especially on my bed." He screwed his handsome face into a grimace. "What's causing that?"

"Anal sacs," I replied casually.

He did a double take, looking confused and, frankly, shocked. I paused a moment. What was the problem? Oh my God, I thought! "No," I explained, "anal sacs—*s-a-c-s*—anal sacs. They're little glands inside the anus; they can get impacted."

"Oh, yes," he graciously replied, taking a sip of his tea. "Sacs."

My whole face burned. I could not look at this man. The words *sacs* and *sex* sound a lot alike if spoken quickly.

A Mounting Problem (BRIAN)

The instant I rang the doorbell, a small dog exploded into frenzied barking. The gentle voice of an elderly woman chided him. "Maxwell Lentz, you stop that." Maxwell stopped nothing. "Maxie, sweetie, Maxie . . ." The woman gave up and opened the door.

The buffed hardwood floors peeked out from the edges of what used to be lush Oriental carpeting. A wonderful collection of African art graced the walls and the smell of freshly brewed coffee permeated the air. This would have been a near perfect moment had not Maxwell, a determined Yorkshire Terrier, latched onto my leg with the express purpose of defiling my shin. For a small dog, he had a strong grip.

Mrs. Lentz clapped her hands in glee. "Oh, good!" she exclaimed. "He likes you! He's hugging you!"

I looked down at the apple of her eye, who was working toward a crescendo of thrusts. He stepped from one back foot to another, trying to get higher up my leg. "He's not hugging me!" I interjected. "He's humping me, and it's disgusting." I gave my leg a light shake, hoping this would dislodge my little Don Juan. My movement made him clamp down harder. The thrusts were so fast now that I was a bit concerned he might hurt himself.

I bent down swiftly, grabbed him firmly by the midsection, and lifted him free. Max continued the movements for several seconds while suspended above the ancient Oriental. "Mrs. Lentz, the first thing we need to do is put him on lead, and the second thing we need to do is teach you the difference between hugging and what just happened."

"Oh, fine," she replied, handing me Max's red leather lead, which matched his collar. Maxwell Lentz was clearly a much-cherished companion, despite his bad manners. "Would you like a cup of coffee?" Mrs. Lentz inquired, smiling. I smiled back. Max was the only one in the room who was not amused.

Hotel Hideaway (BRIAN)

This Long Island couple could no longer afford their dog. Paying for dog food, vet care, and toys wasn't the problem; it was the extras that were killing them.

They called me in for help. Their five-year-old Chesapeake Bay Retriever, Turk, stared at me coolly as I spoke with his owners, Mike and Betty Bradshaw.

"Turk's really a good dog most of the time." This phrase is always the precursor to the real problems.

"Okay, but what about the rest of the time?"

"He's protective," Betty said.

"Protective how?" I pressed. This was going to be good—they were stalling on the answer.

"Well . . ." She hesitated, glancing at Mike. Mike stepped in. "He doesn't like us being . . . intimate." Betty blushed. This is not an uncommon problem in animals who feel that they are in charge of the house. In fact, at first many people think this is cute behavior. They laugh when the dog squeezes between them when they hug or when he climbs up on the couch to sit between them. But in the Bradshaws' case, Turk took it to new heights.

"What does he do?"

"He becomes a wild man. He barks, scratches at the door. Completely loses it. It's gotten so bad that we don't 'do' anything in the house anymore."

"Not in the house?" Momentarily, my mind raced to the other possibilities—the garage, the tree house?

"No, we sneak out the bedroom window and go down to the motel on the corner."

"That's a creative solution—time consuming, expensive, but creative."

"Expensive!" Mike sighed. "You bet it is. Not only do

we have to pay for a full night but we've had to replace three bedroom doors, as well."

Doesn't He Need To? (SARAH)

The session was going well. It was a pleasant fall day; our center on West Seventy-fifth Street was cool. It was the kind of day that dogs enjoy. The client was new— an attractive fashion designer, and her burly adolescent unneutered male Pit Bull Terrier.

In the early 1990s, Pits, as they are known to their friends, were fighting some very bad press. Owned for some of the wrong reasons by some of the wrong people, this breed was in the news far too often for violence against humans. Such aggression toward people, virtually unheard-of in the past, was recently on the rise in New York City due to poor breeding and poor rearing practices. This being true, the sight of this tail-thumping young male was a pleasant surprise.

But Pits are a powerful breed with an often-built-in desire to scrap with other animals, so I launched into my normal set of questions for the owner of a powerful dog. I did not want to miss anything.

"Do you have any trouble with him growling at other dogs?" I asked.

"Oh, no. He loves other dogs." I sighed with relief. This was mighty unusual for a hormonal adolescent Pit Bull.

"Do you have any trouble with him growling at people?"

"No. Never!" she said emphatically as she stroked his large head.

"Do you have any trouble with him being possessive over toys or food?" I was just being thorough now. It always amazes me how people will tell me emphatically that their dog is not aggressive, then admit two minutes later that he growls if you approach his food bowl.

"He's a love," she said, looking at me as if I were slightly daft to be missing her point here that he was a wonderful dog.

"Excellent." I grinned at her. This was splendid. "Okay, for the record. Do you have any trouble with mounting?"

"Oh my, no," she said. "I just use a big bath towel."

My pencil hovered above the paper. An unwanted image flooded my mind. "Excuse me?"

"Well, my pants were getting to be such a mess, I just cover myself with a towel."

"Ugh." I made a face. The idea of that dog having his way with her crisply pressed, designer pant legs stunned me. I slid into a mantra of nos as I recovered from surprise.

"But I have to use the towel." As if the towel was the problem.

"You can't do that. You can't let him do that." I jabbed my pencil at her with every syllable.

"I thought he needed to . . . relieve himself." She looked puzzled. What was I so upset about?

"Needed to? Needed to went out in seventh grade." I took a breath, consciously making an effort to calm down. "He does not need to. Allowing him to do this will cause problems down the line."

"You think so?" She looked so perplexed. She would make some man very happy with this accommodating attitude.

"I don't *think* so," I stated, leaning toward her. "I *know* so. It will promote aggression. This is already a breed that tends toward pushiness. He doesn't need this to help him along."

"I thought the release would make him more mellow."

"Listen, he doesn't think of it as release; he thinks he's having sex with you." That hit home. She paled slightly, then turned crimson. "Ooh," she said softly, drawing out the word. She looked down at her dog with dawning comprehension. No more free rides for him.

Is This Normal? (BRIAN)

I've got a really big problem." The man's voice was intense and worried. He was a psychiatrist, which meant that he would probably make a terrible dog-training student.

"What's going on?" I inquired.

"Well, I have a brother and sister dog," he began. "They are seven months old. They are doing it in the kitchen."

"Doing it? What do you mean?" It could be a house-breaking issue—maybe chewing.

"I mean *doing* it. Having sex. Right now!" His voice rose higher.

"Okay—are they neutered?" I hoped this would be a yes.

"Yes, yes, they're neutered, but," he sputtered into the phone, "they're *doing it!* That's . . . that's . . ." He paused for a second, then continued with clear disdain in his voice: "That's incest!"

Chastity Dog (SARAH)

Training dogs is an amazing profession. Not only do you get invited into people's homes to hear the most intimate details of their lives but you also get to tell them exactly what they should do. To top it off, they pay. Amazing.

One couple who called me sticks in my mind. They lived in a perfectly nice prewar building on the Upper West Side of Manhattan, near Columbia University. After an hour or so of working with them and their shy Toy Fox Terrier, Bounce, the truth came out.

"Ah, we're having a problem with Bounce. . . ."

"A problem?" I responded.

"She likes to sleep with us. . . ." The woman's voice drifted off as she looked at her partner.

"Okay, lots of dogs do."

"Well, she doesn't like it when we are . . . well . . . intimate."

"Doesn't like it?"

"She paws at us and cries. It's very upsetting." The woman was quite earnest. It was clear from her tone and the eye contact that "upsetting" actually translated into "stopped everything cold."

"When did this behavior start?" I expected to hear it was a few weeks ago.

"About a year ago."

"A year?" I considered this for a second or two. "You *are* patient. If I were you, I would put her in her crate in another room, close the door of that room, close the door of the bedroom, turn on the stereo, and forget about her. This is her problem; there is no need to make it yours." A Toy Fox Terrier can be mighty cute, but not cute enough to keep me from having sex for a year.

The couple exchanged glances. One was understandably excited and slightly smug in a loving but definite "I told you so" way. The other was near panic.

"Crate time isn't going to hurt her one bit," I said reassuringly, but I could see that this was not going to be a solution. The fact was, I couldn't help in this situation. The dog had become the excuse, but she wasn't really the problem. What they needed was a therapist, not a dog trainer.

I Hate to Ask, But . . . (BRIAN)

Being a dog trainer makes you string words together that you never thought would be mingling in a sentence. For example, "Drinking out of the toilet is perfectly normal." Or: "If you continue to feed him under the bed, he will stay there."

No matter how long you do this job, if you're doing in-home work, you are being challenged with new and sometimes awkward situations. Two of our favorite clients, whom we both respect and adore, have precipitated more than one of these sentences. One of the most embarrassing happened when their Airedale, Chadwick, was about eleven months old.

As we were drinking tea, sitting on a couch that no doubt cost more than any car I have ever owned, they mentioned that Chadwick had recently been destructive. Now, this was surprising, as he had no history of it and was rarely alone enough to be destructive.

"What happened?" I inquired, stirring some milk into my Earl Grey.

"So odd," Joan responded. "He ripped up our sheets."

"Has he done this before?" I was stalling a bit, hopeful that this was not what I feared it was.

"Why no, though sometimes he has sniffed them a lot."

"Ah, well. He is a teenager now." I continued as tactfully as I could. "I have to ask you something that I would not normally ask, but I promise it is relevant to the problem." Joan looked surprised but nodded.

"Did you have . . . well, relations the night before?"

Not blinking an eye, Joan laughed. "As a matter of fact, yes."

"That's it, then. He's reaching sexual maturity and all

sorts of bells and whistles are going off in his head. He should grow through this phase, but in the meantime, change the sheets and lock him out of the room when you can't supervise him."

GIFTED CANINES

Psychic Companions (BRIAN)

Barbara Woodhouse was a big believer in human/canine mental connections. She constantly counseled, "Picture it clearly in your mind. See it exactly as you want it to be."

Athletic coaches, a few medical professionals, and most positive thinkers might just say she was preaching imagery for success. But Barbara believed, and had ample personal anecdotal proof, that dogs can be connected to their people in a profound, and as-yet-unexplained, telepathic way.

It was her belief that animals think in pictures. If you are focused and completely clear about what you want from your dog, the dog can pick that up from you.

Most of us have had that experience with our pets. British scientists supported this common dog-owner experience by testing dogs about being able to anticipate their owner's arrival home. Most dogs could do it to one extent or another. One little terrier mix was gifted. Change the time, change the route home, change the vehicle used, and still he was up and sitting at the front window, waiting ten to fifteen minutes before his owner walked up the front steps.

Some of these experiences may look like ESP but are probably something less glamorous. Special dogs are now being trained to predict their owner's oncoming epileptic seizures. Knowing that a seizure is on the way allows the owner time to get to a reasonably private and safe place before it hits. This offers some welcome control over a most misunderstood and frightening event.

How do dogs do this? Chances are their brilliant noses are the answer. Chemical changes probably take place in the body prior to the onset of a seizure that are easy for a dog to detect, once he understands their significance.

Other dogs have developed skills at sniffing out skin cancers. One high-strung Miniature Dachshund carefully, deeply, and persistently licks the very spot on her owner's head that hurts during her migraines.

But ESP? Absolutely! I know it's true. I'll just wait for science to catch up to prove it. How can you argue with the following story?

One day, Sarah is working in the kitchen and Mica, an Australian Shepherd pup, is playing at her feet. Caras is asleep against the back door. Mica starts to chew a sneaker. Sarah says, "Leave it." Mica cocks her head, looks at Sarah, then goes back to the sneaker. After this interchange is repeated a few times, Sarah realizes it is neither effective nor productive. While staring at Mica and without moving or speaking, Sarah thinks, I need a replacement object here. That artificial sheepskin toy would be perfect.

Caras wakes up with a start. He runs into the living room, gets the toy, comes back, drops it in front of Mica, and puts his paws in Sarah's lap. This is especially odd because Caras hates sharing that toy with puppies.

Hm . . .

Another dog we know lives with children. This animal is well socialized with kids, enjoying their company more than that of adults. Actually, that's not quite accurate; it's more like he craves their company. One day, while his owner and her kids were out in the backyard, one of the neighborhood boys, around age fourteen or fifteen, came into the yard to say hello.

This child-loving, people-loving dog stepped between his family and this boy and growled. His shocked owner scolded him harshly, then banished him inside the house. Months later, the neighborhood discovered that this troubled young man had been molesting younger children in the local woods for months.

Hm . . .

Many people I know, especially women, trust their dogs implicitly. If their normally friendly dog doesn't like someone, they take the dog's word for it. So all you hopeful suitors out there, bring some biscuits with you when you meet the dog. It may be a more important test to pass than meeting her parents.

My old Rottweiler, Beau, and I were quite interwoven. One evening, after a rather raucous party, I lay sleeping in the pool house. Beau was snoozing in the main house with a mutual friend. The main house was several hundred feet up a hill and behind thick shrubbery, away from the pool. Beau, being upstairs in a bedroom on the far side of the main house, was quite a distance from me.

Late, maybe 2:00 or 3:00 A.M., several of my friends decided I needed a late-night swim. I was strongly against the idea. My friends were laughing and carrying on; I was silent. I was intent on freeing myself. I was also losing the battle. They almost had me to the pool edge when they were blocked by a dark form.

Beau stood between me and the pool, every hair on his body bristling, slowly expanding, as only an enraged Rottweiler can. In the darkness, you could see his two long white canine teeth flash as he raised his lips.

My friends set me down. Once I was upright, I called him to me. Trotting over with the springy step of a happy dog, he greeted everyone. He was not a dog who held a grudge; he simply would not permit harm to come to me. That was his job in life and he did it well. My question is always: How did he know I needed him? That part, I will never discover. He just knew; he always knew.

Canine Nightingale (SARAH)

The joints on her hands were swollen. Her fingers bent almost ninety degrees sideways. Emily walked with special wide shoes. I imagined her toes looked very much like her fingers. With every movement she made, I grimaced inside. She lived with permanent, incredible, unimaginable pain.

But here she was in my beginner's class at Orange Community Pet Hospital with her adorable American Cocker Spaniel. Amazingly, this woman always had a smile. It took her a bit longer to do many of the exercises, but she did them happily. She adored her pup.

During free play time, this pup was a classic little outgoing hellion. She teased the other pups, raced around the room, ears flapping behind her, greeting everyone by leaping at and on them. Her tail never stopped. *She* never stopped.

But when Emily picked up the lead, this pup seemed to mature several years. She sat calmly at Emily's feet. She walked with great care by her side, looking up, checking every few steps. She never pulled or jumped. She did not show any signs of stress or fear, as a pup who had been tripped over or harshly scolded for misbehavior might. If this pup knew anything, she knew that her rambunctious behavior would pain her companion, and that, clearly, was the last thing she wanted to do.

Toby's Vigil (BRIAN)

Toby was a typical young Basenji. These graceful little dogs are active with a capital A! While the breed is barkless, they are not noiseless. Depending on their mood, they chortle, yodel, howl, and scream. They tend toward feats of athleticism such as climbing onto bookshelves or the dining room table.

When Paul, his owner, developed full-blown AIDS and spent more and more time in bed, Toby kept him company. The exuberant young dog would lie for hours with his head resting motionless across his friend's chest. One of Paul's few great pleasures was to play with Toby. He would touch the dog's whiskers, which Toby hated, causing Toby to wage mock battle with Paul in slow, careful movements. Toby never left a mark on him. When Paul felt like doing little else, he felt like playing with Toby.

As the illness progressed, Toby's vigil intensified. He had to be lifted from the bed and carried outside when it was time for his walks. Outside, he would quickly relieve himself, then race back to the house and scratch at the front door. Once in, he would spring upstairs, vault back into bed, and stretch out gently against Paul's ravaged body. There Toby would stay until he was forced, yet again, to leave his charge.

In the end, the very end, Paul went to the hospital. In the last few hours of his life, in delirium and pain, in a hospital bed miles from his home, Paul played with an imaginary Toby. In his heart and mind, the little dog was with him, which is clearly what Toby would have wanted.

Just a Chance (SARAH)

Anne, an Australian Shepherd breeder and friend, called last night. Her oldest male, Ashley, who was my Caras's father, had to be put to sleep last week. His quality of life was gone; he was frightened and confused most of the time. It was a horrible decision for her, but she made it. It was the last thing she could do for him.

Later that grim day, she let all her other dogs out for their constitutional. When she called them back in, Chance, an Ashley son and the pack's second in command, was missing. Chance is a reliable dog, deeply attached to Anne. He never wanders.

Anne leapt into her car. Driving up and down her dead-end road, she called for him. He was nowhere to be seen. On her third pass along the road, she spotted him. He was crossing a bridge, more than a mile from home, headed toward the busier roads. Stopping the car, she yelled to him, "Chance! What are you doing?" He stopped, turning his chiseled black-and-white face toward her.

"It was the strangest thing," she told me later. "I heard him. I knew. He told me, Looking for Ashley." Her voice caught in her throat. "I tried to explain to him what had happened. I don't know if he understood any of it. But he hasn't gone looking for him since." We both stayed silent for a few moments on the phone.

"Great dogs you have there," I told her, reaching down to pat Caras. "Really great dogs."

T. Time (BRIAN)

If there is reincarnation, I am sure that T. and I knew each other in past lives. We were so inseparable in this one.

After I went off to Iowa State to begin study for prevet, he saved my family a lot of long-distance phone calls. About three days before I would arrive home from college, he would begin making funny kinds of grunting, whining sounds. As the drive home was a long one, over one thousand miles, this behavior generally correlated to my starting my trip home.

At first, my mom didn't know what to make of these noises, but over time she came to connect them with what always came next. Two hours before I pulled up the driveway, T. parked himself by the back door. No one and nothing could move him.

When I got out of my car, T. was always the first to greet me. Someday, if there is a heaven, he will meet me again, after aggravating St. Peter with three days' worth of chortling, moaning, and grunting at the Pearly Gates.

Search and Rescue (BRIAN)

Many estimates float around about how much more sensitive a dog's nose is than a human's, but none is really much help. The canine nose is not just more sensitive; it is completely different. We nasally challenged humans can not really grasp how different, any more than someone born blind can fully grasp color. It's impossible.

In search and rescue (SAR), humans and canines team up to use both species' best characteristics to bring about miracles. We humans are excellent conceptual thinkers; we make up the game plan, discuss it with the other dog/

handler teams, make decisions, and then let the dogs do their stuff.

Typical calls for these heroes involve children or elderly people lost in the woods, or adults who have wandered off for some reason, usually a grim one. In the fall, hunters seeking communion with the great outdoors get a bit more than they bargained for. The calls come at all times of day and night, and these volunteers drop everything to help.

One SAR volunteer, Joe, told this story.

"The first time I went out with Rhett [his eighteen-month-old male red bloodhound], it was at night. A man was missing. His car had been found nearby. Rhett and I started to search our assigned area. Just a few minutes in, he hit some scent and dragged me along for quite a while. I began to wonder, Is he on the scent of a raccoon or deer or something? After fifteen minutes or so, he came to a dead stop in the middle of the woods. I flashed my light around—nothing but bushes and big old trees. Not a sign.

"I took him off a ways and started him again. Right back to that spot and those trees. I shook my head. All this work, all these hours of training, and he hauls me along after some kind of animal. I decided to call it a night.

"I reported our failure to the search coordinator and went on home, really disappointed.

"At daybreak, the man was still missing, so I went back with Rhett and hit our zone again. Again, he made a beeline to that little grove. I couldn't understand. In frustration, I threw my hands up and looked to the sky, and there the man was. He'd hung himself in the biggest tree in the grove. Rhett had brought me right to him, directly underneath him.

"Now who's stupid?"

In olfactory skills, we will never understand, never mind compete with, a canine nose.

The other extraordinary work these dogs do is water-rescue work. Newfoundlands were bred to leap into the water to assist drowning people. But the SAR dogs do the emotionally vital work of locating the bodies of people who did not have a Newfoundland around to help.

I wondered how these animals were trained for their work. Not surprisingly, scuba gear is involved. First, a person lies on the shore, half in the water and half out. When the dog finds the person, she gets a piece of hot dog, a favorite toy to play with, or some other treat that excites that particular dog. The next time, the person is more in the water. This continues until the person is just submerged. Then the dog is put into a rowboat and rowed over the body of the diver. (It has to be a rowboat, as an outboard motor's strong fuel smell might compromise the dog's abilities.) Somehow, the dog can smell the body and proceeds to signal by barking and pawing at the water.

After training, dogs can be rowed back and forth over a lake and will signal when they are over drowning victims' bodies submerged in many, many feet of water. In fact, just recently, an SAR dog located the arm of a young girl; it had been amputated in a horrific motorboat accident. How else could we have possibly found that little arm?

Caras—TV Star (SARAH)

The camera is attached to the cameraman with a harness full of metal arms, cables, and joints. Three or more cables are attached to the camera itself and a separate guy in jeans walks beside the cameraman, making sure the cables stay out of his way. The soundman, with his huge black foam-covered mike suspended from a long black boom, stands beside those two. The director for this television special, destined for Japanese TV, flanks them, giving directions. The sound assistant is organizing wires, cables, and other gear. This whole mechanical/human pod walks backward down Fifth Avenue, less than three feet in front of Caras's face, most of them staring at him. The camera is held down at his face level, looming closer, then pulling away as certain shots come and go.

It is one of the busiest street corners in Manhattan—Fifty-seventh and Fifth. Across the street is Tiffany; Trump Tower rears its shiny facade next to Tiffany; FAO Schwarz is a block north, Rockefeller Center just a few blocks south—it is one of the most New York of New York areas and it is swarming with life. Hundreds of people are shopping, sight-seeing, going to or coming from work; bike messengers whiz by at breakneck speeds; buses stop to regurgitate passengers, then inhale more. The sidewalk is mobbed.

My job is to have Caras walk down the sidewalk, paying no attention to the chaos around him or the cable-covered human mass walking directly in front of him. Simple job? Not quite.

The camera is set up, the sound is set up, the people hired to keep all the passersby out of the shot are in position, and the woman who walks behind me, guiding me from the rear as I walk backward in front of Caras, instructing him, is present. Ready, set, action. Off we go. Caras works perfectly, but the camera guy stumbled a bit. Cut!

Return to start. Fuss with equipment. I play with Caras between shots to keep him relaxed. Ready, set, action! This one was smooth except for the businessman who stopped to watch directly in the frame. Cut!

Back to start. Ready, set, action! Caras loses his concentration and wanders off to sniff a tree. Cut!

Ready, set, action. A bus backfires. Cut!

Ready, set, action. An escapee from the fashion industry rolls a noisy rack full of clothing past. I am proud that Caras stays focused, but the *clocha-clocha-clocha* of the wheels on the sidewalk ruins the sound. Cut!

This is the nature of low-budget shooting on location in the city. After almost an hour and a half, the director has what he wants.

Next, they want a shot of Caras crossing Fifth Avenue. This is a harder shot for me. Caras starts off sitting at the curb when the light changes; then he gets up, walks across the street, and continues down the sidewalk on the other side, past a hot-dog vendor.

This single segment takes another hour and a half, which

is actually light speed when you consider that we have to work everything around when we have a WALK signal. Caras probably works fifteen minutes; the rest of the time is spent waiting for the light, the equipment to get set up, horns to stop blaring, people to stop pointing, or police cars to go by. Caras does quite well, stopping only once to air scent the hot dogs, a shot the director loves. He uses that in the final cut.

The hardest one of the day is the last one. Caras has to walk into the frame, sniff a tree, then walk out of the frame. Easy? Easy at first, but once a dog has sniffed a tree a couple of times, he pretty much has all the information he needs. Just try to get him to sniff it again.

The first time, he sniffs the tree perfectly, but then he ducks behind it, ruining his exit. After that, I have to make the tree interesting. Cheese rubbed into the bark—out of the camera's view—works pretty well once I get the hang of how much to use. Too much caused Caras to stop and lick it, making him look as if he is eating the tree. Too little and he doesn't stop at all. I know this won't work for long—there is not enough mystery in it to keep him going back.

In the end, after a couple more days shooting in Times Square, Columbus Circle, and a grooming parlor in Greenwich Village, everything is completed. In the final show, Caras trots around town, looking debonair, while a husky Australian-accented male voice speaks for him. No one would ever guess how complicated it can be to make things look so easy.

A Lesson in Character (BRIAN)

Helping out at a local Long Island veterinary clinic was one of my first real jobs, a job I wanted desperately to do well. When I was an adolescent, when neither home nor school was much fun, animals were my sure haven.

My duties were not glamorous. Entry-level animal care seldom is. It's mostly taking care of what goes into an animal and what comes out of an animal, the latter making up most of the workload. Sometimes, I got to help the vet with actual treatments. That was the best.

One day, one task, and one particular animal are burned in my mind forever. She was a little Beagle, a Beagle who had been allowed to run loose. She had been hit by a car, got caught somehow underneath, and was dragged. When she arrived at the clinic, her entire left side was embedded with gravel, glass, and dirt.

As sometimes happens at any medical facility, emergencies come in bunches. The doctor and his technician had to open up another poor animal to save his life. That left me with the Beagle. My job was to pick out the hundreds of shards of glass and bits of gravel from this little dog's mangled body.

She lay on the table, unanesthetized, motionless. I spoke to her softly as I went about my business as gently as I could. Her flesh lay exposed in angry, yawning wounds. Her beautiful black-white-and-tan coat was curled back onto itself, like shirtsleeves pushed up.

As I pulled knives of glass out of her muscle, she would whine softly. Sometimes I had to lift flaps of flesh in order to reach some dirt underneath. If my hand happened to move past her muzzle, she would, with effort, turn to lick me. Then she would lay her head back down, closing her doelike brown eyes slightly, ready for me to continue.

And I did continue, with reverence for what she offered me that day. Such a great spirit resided in that little hound marked body: She showed more character in that afternoon than some people do in a lifetime.

Many experiences shaped me into the trainer I am today, that little hound included. I can accept a lot of things, but not the mishandling of an animal. Their trust in us is too complete to abuse it with irresponsible ownership, cruel methods, or simple thoughtlessness.

Other Resources from Brian Kilcommons and Sarah Wilson

For information call 1-800-457-PETS.

Good Owners, Great Dogs—A training manual for humans and their canine companions. Over 100,000 copies in use. This comprehensive training guide for all canine ages and problems is fun to read and has more than 300 pictures of 45 different breeds. Covers puppy selection and training, housebreaking, chewing, running away, jumping, all forms of aggression, adult dog training, and canine care. If you have a dog-related question, this book has the answer. Methods are, of course, humane, effective, commonsense, and fun!

Good Owners, Great Dogs (Video)—This is the companion video to our best-selling book of the same title. This video brings the book to life and makes understanding techniques more comprehensive. Most of the dogs used in this video were taken straight from shelters. The video covers basic commands/manners such as controlling jumping, barking, stealing food, and destructive chewing. Housebreaking and crate training are also included. This is an excellent way to learn the proper voice intonation and handling skills. Emphasizes praise and teaching.

Good Owners, Great Cats—The most comprehensive book on cat and kitten care we could create. Everything is covered, from understanding your cat to curing destructive scratching, from litterbox training to eliminating spraying, from stopping ankle biting to introducing a new cat to your household. As always, methods are humane and effective. This book, written by cat lovers for cat lovers, will make you smile while you learn.

Childproofing Your Dog—This book is light reading, yet gives you all the information you need to teach your dog to be reliable around children before a child comes into your life. It's never too late to train your dog, but the sooner you start, the safer your child/dog relationship will be. This book focuses on the need to educate the dog about what children are likely to do prior to the kids' doing it. Designed to be quick, informative reading for busy parents (and parents-to-be) who have little spare time.

The Good Owners, Great Dogs Newsletter—Our new quarterly publication is aimed at providing valuable information in the areas of training and behavior, health and nutrition, product review, and more.

Mutts . . . America's Dog—The encyclopedia of mixed-breed dogs: Who they are, what they do, how they do it, and what kind of companions they will make in your life. This book profiles over a hundred mixed-breed dogs with a special emphasis on their trainability and how they fit into human families.

Come and visit us at our website; it's useful and informative and always just a click of the mouse away. You'll find us at www.greatpets.com

more . . .

MUTTS: AMERICA'S DOGS
A Guide to Choosing, Loving, and Living with Our Most Popular Canine
by Brian Kilcommons and Michael Capuzzo

Mutts is an encyclopedia and a celebration of the pets Americans love best. Delving into the temperaments, personalities, and skills of over a hundred mixed-breed dogs, it tells you how to choose the best dog or puppy for your family and how to train and care for your crossbreed. Full of wonderful photographs and sometimes heartbreaking and often hilarious firstperson accounts of these fascinating animals, this guide is informative, fun to read, and bursting with mutt love.